James Milligan

A Book of Poems for People Under 4ft 2

Nightingale Books

NIGHTINGALE PAPERBACK

**© Copyright 2025
James Milligan**

The right of James Milligan to be identified as author of this work has been asserted by him in accordance with the Copyright, Designs and Patents Act 1988.

All Rights Reserved

No reproduction, copy or transmission of this publication may be made without written permission.
No paragraph of this publication may be reproduced, copied or transmitted save with the written permission of the publisher, or in accordance with the provisions of the Copyright Act 1956 (as amended).

Any person who commits any unauthorised act in relation to this publication may be liable to criminal prosecution and civil claims for damages.

A CIP catalogue record for this title is available from the British Library.

ISBN 978-1-78788-066-5

*Nightingale Books is an imprint of
Pegasus Elliot MacKenzie Publishers Ltd.
www.pegasuspublishers.com*

First Published in 2025

**Nightingale Books
Sheraton House Castle Park
Cambridge England**

Printed & Bound in Great Britain

Illustrations by

Kourosh Edelat

https://linktr.ee
/kedartstudio?ut...

Foreword

This book is dedicated to all the children of our beautiful world. Could you all please very kindly stop getting bigger, and DO NOT grow up into big, smelly, hairy, long toe-nailed adults.

Backwards

This book is dedicated to all the children of our beautiful world. Could you all please very kindly stop getting bigger, and DO NOT grow up into big, smelly, hairy, long toe-nailed adults.

'Here is a nice book for you.

With poems, pictures, and a few jokes too.

It's not serious or meant for studies or exams,

But just for fun and playing around.

So forget about school just for now,

And spend some time joking and reading aloud.'

Table of Content

The Policeman's Hat	9
The Octopus Captain	11
The Fat Bats of Pookiniki	13
Matilda the Python	15
Hippo Soup	17
The Lion and the Traffic Warden	19
The Best Ship	21
Fredericks the Frog	23
The Horseham Express	25
Great Ape	27
Philbert the Jamaican Flea	29
The Lion and the Naughty Boy	30
The Sergeant Major	33
Clever Emma	35
The Great Fart of 2002	37
The Toilet Brush	39
Cannibal Values	40
Bee Work	41
The Jellyfish Tea Party	43
Fisherman Kelly	45
Kevin the Camel	47
Wind Holes	49
Smelly Wellies	51
The Lion and the Maths Teacher	53
The Pup Sherry	55
Molly the Mosquito	57
Fairy Spy Cakes	59
Colin the Crocodile	61
The Worried Professor	63
Volcano	65
The Lion and the Geography Teacher	67
Percy the Penguin	69
Dave the Goalkeeper	71
Hubert Humperbump	73
The Prince with Big Feet	75
Football	77
A Vegetarian Wolf in Gloucester	79
The Rugby Scrum	81
The Ping and The Pong	83
The Kings Coronation	85
The Potchkin's Alphabet	86
About the author	88

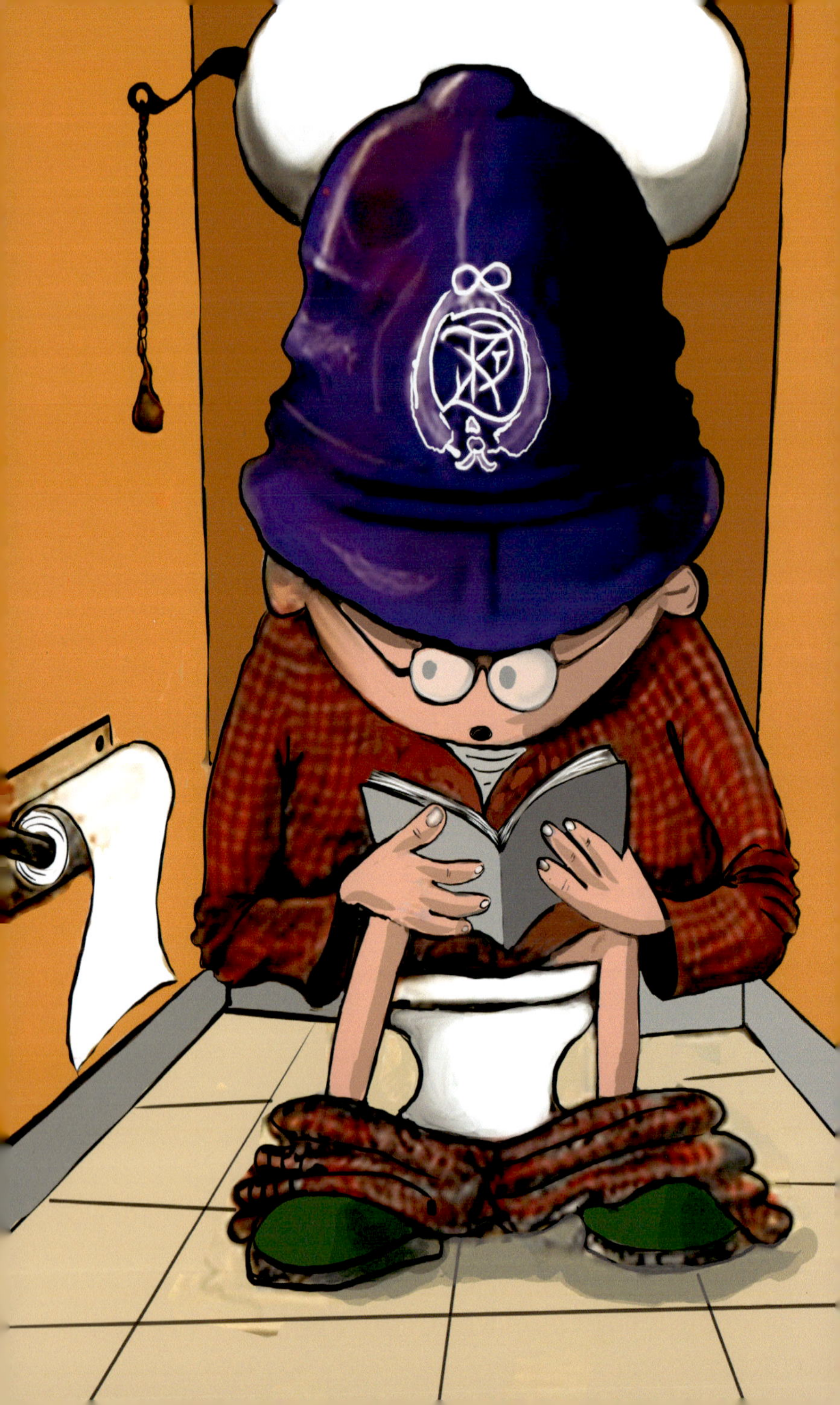

The Policeman's Hat

Our town's policeman wears a big blue hat.
He is short, wears glasses and is really rather fat.
His hat is tall and heavy, but he never takes it off.
Even when he is feeling poorly with a nasty cough.

He wears it when he's out to dinner and asleep in bed.
He wears it so much I think it's glued to his head.
It is on his head all week long and on weekends too.
He even wears it with his trousers down sitting on the loo.

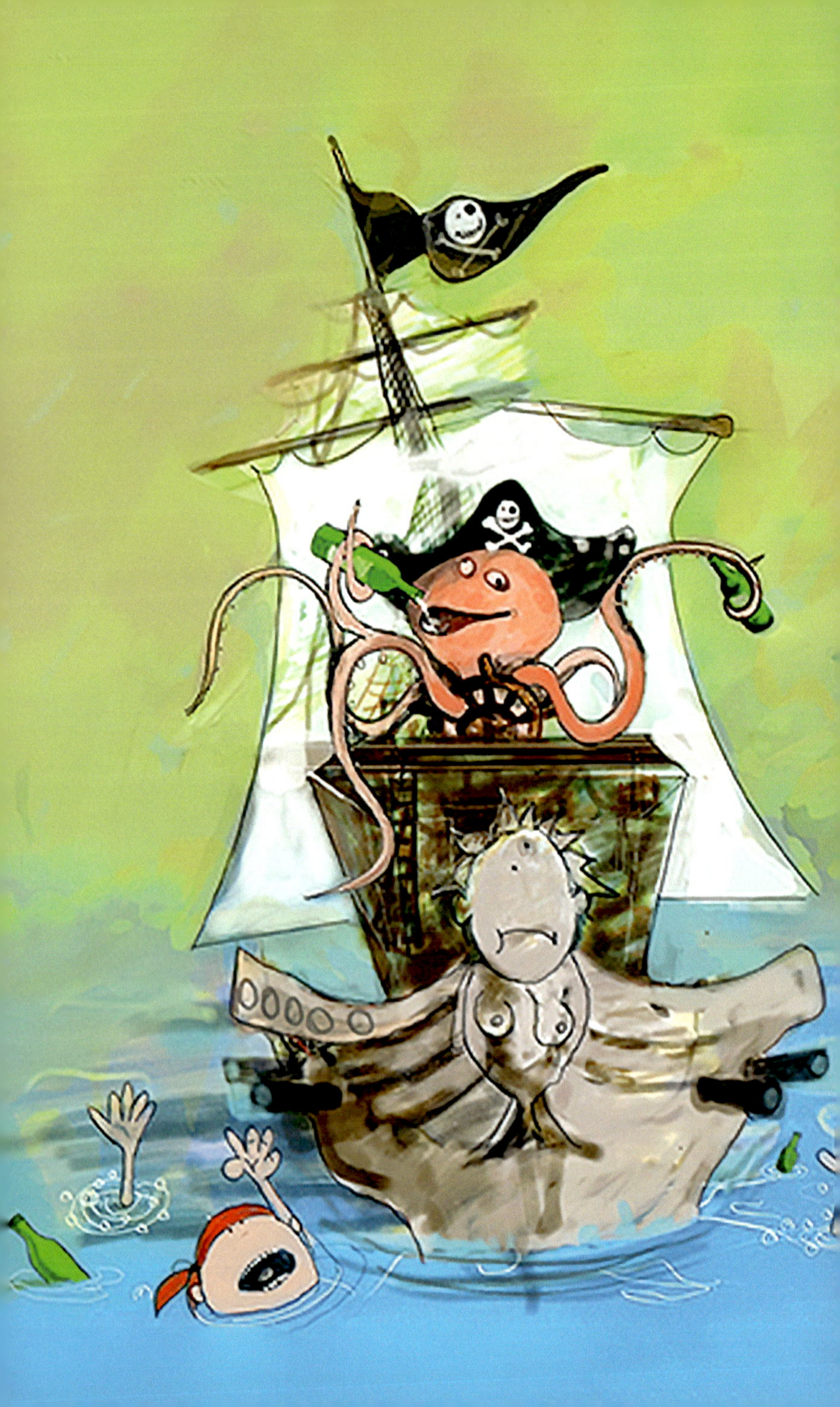

The Octopus Captain

The enormous pirate ship had a big black skull and cross bones sail.
And a wooden mermaid on the front with her fish's tail.
This pirate ship sailed the seven seas and all around the globe.
With a crew of pirate thieves who had a ruthless code.

The captain is tall and rubbery with lots of flailing arms.
He wears a pirate's hat and has very slimy palms.
When the sun shines over this pirate's ship and all is in the light,
You can see the captain is an Octopus man laughing with delight.

He steers the ship all day long drinking lots of rum.
And uses his long tentacles to scratch his itchy bum.
If anyone dares alter his ship's course and plight,
He squirts his black ink at them to give an awful fright.

His crew decide one day upon a dastardly plan.
To get rid of the Octopus captain as quickly as they can.
They sneak behind him late at night while on raging seas.
But the Octopus captain is still awake and scares the men who flee.

He chases them around the ship picking them from the ground.
And throws the pirates overboard never to be found.
A normal captain would be worried with no crew or staff.
But with eight arms he steers his ship, hoists the sail and carries on to laugh.

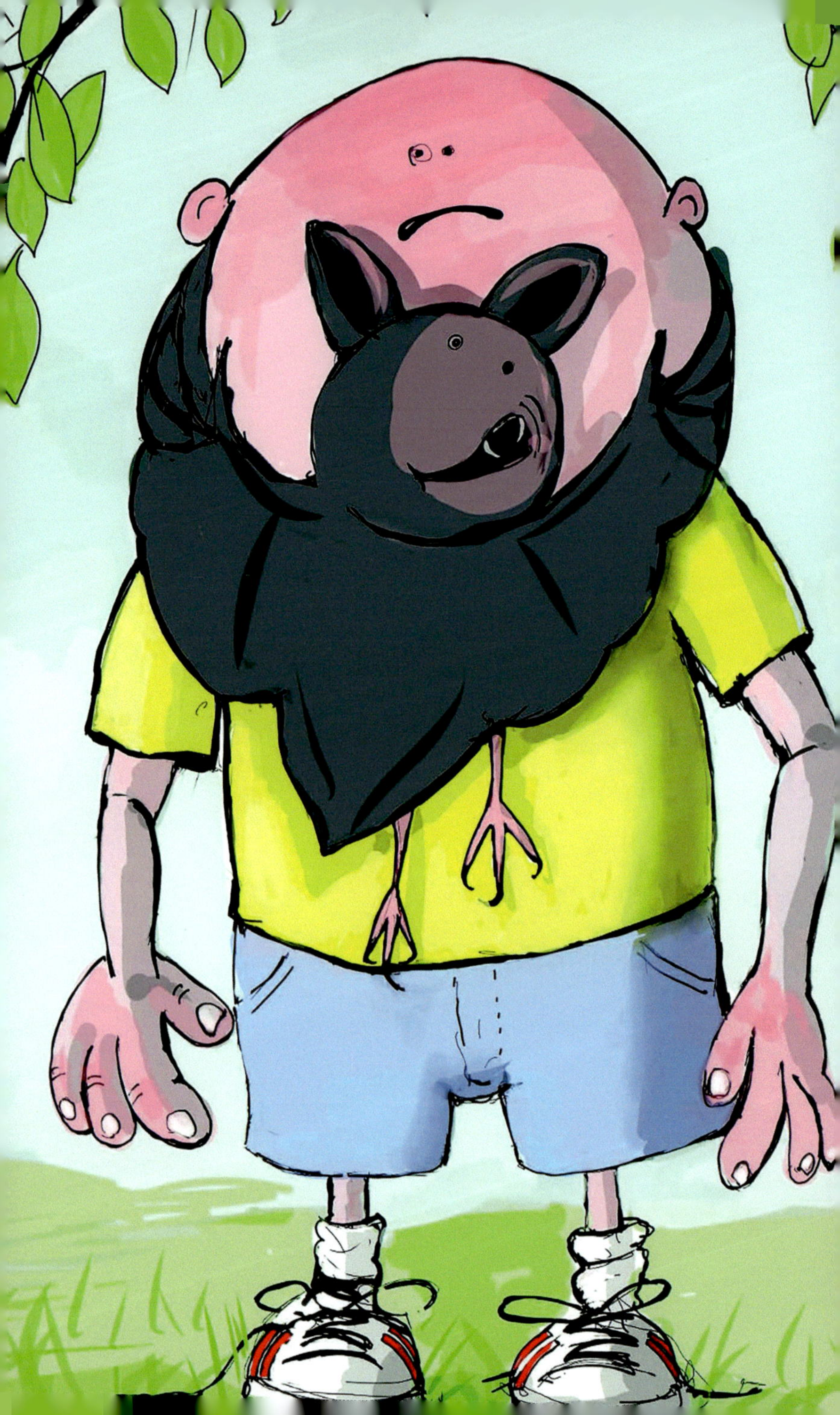

The Fat Bats of Pookiniki

The fat bats of Pookiniki,
Come out late at night to play.
They're so round and plump,
They only fly for five minutes a day.

They swoop down for a cuddle,
If they see you walking by.
And wrap themselves around your face,
They're not at all very shy.

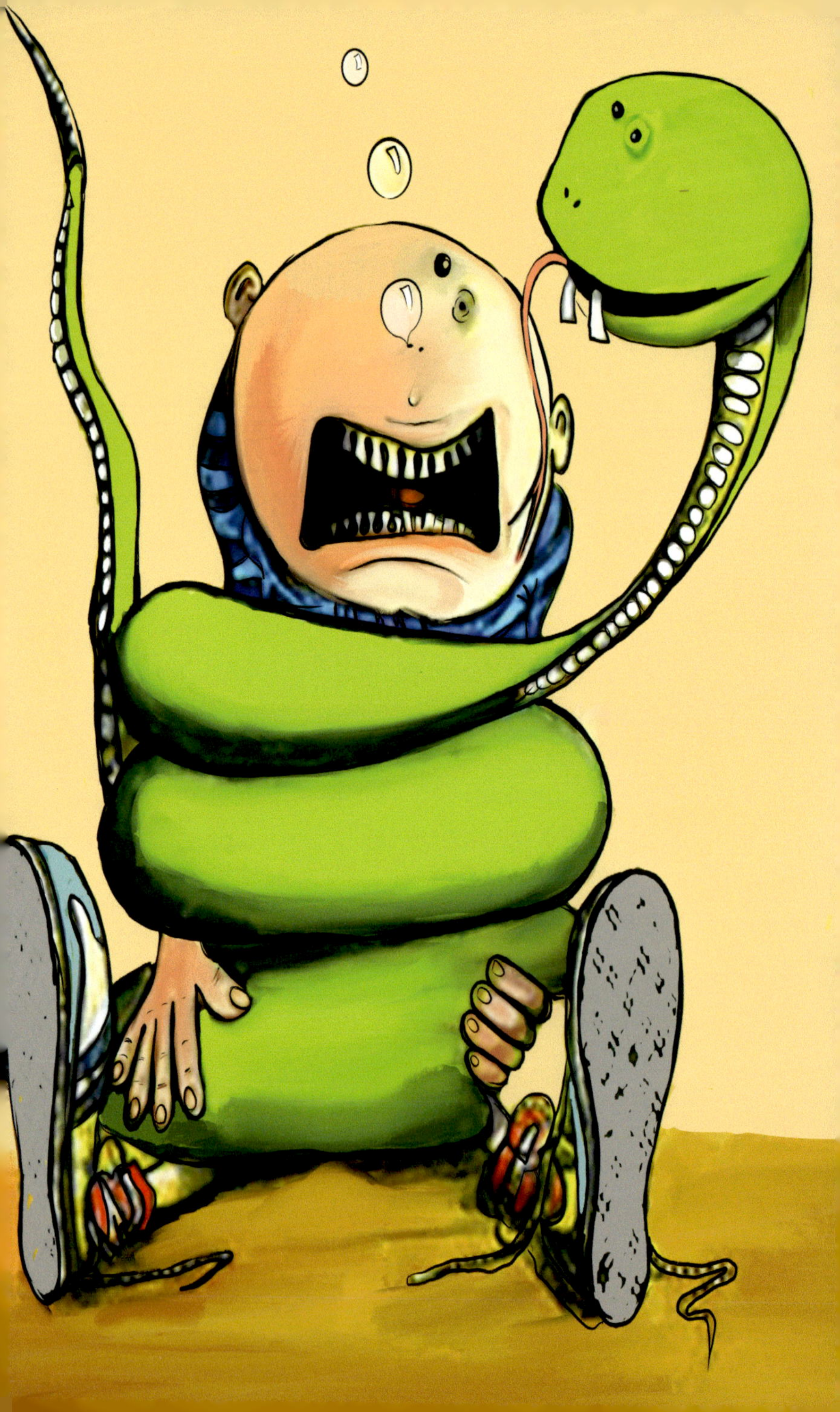

Matilda the Python

My friend Bob is plump and rather round.
Sometimes his belly flops out and scraps along the ground.
He sits down all day eating pies and watching TV,
And only gets up for more food, or an occasional pee.

He owns a big snake called Matilda who is stripy with a white belly.
She sits in her tank at the back of the room looking at Bob watching telly.
Then one day Matilda breaks her tank door and slithers to the floor.
Fat Bob turns in sheer fright scared to his very core.

He tries to run away, but can hardly lift a leg.
He's so fat every move feels like lifting lead.
Matilda catches up easily and wraps around him tight.
She licks her lips, opens wide and swallows poor Bob in one big bite!

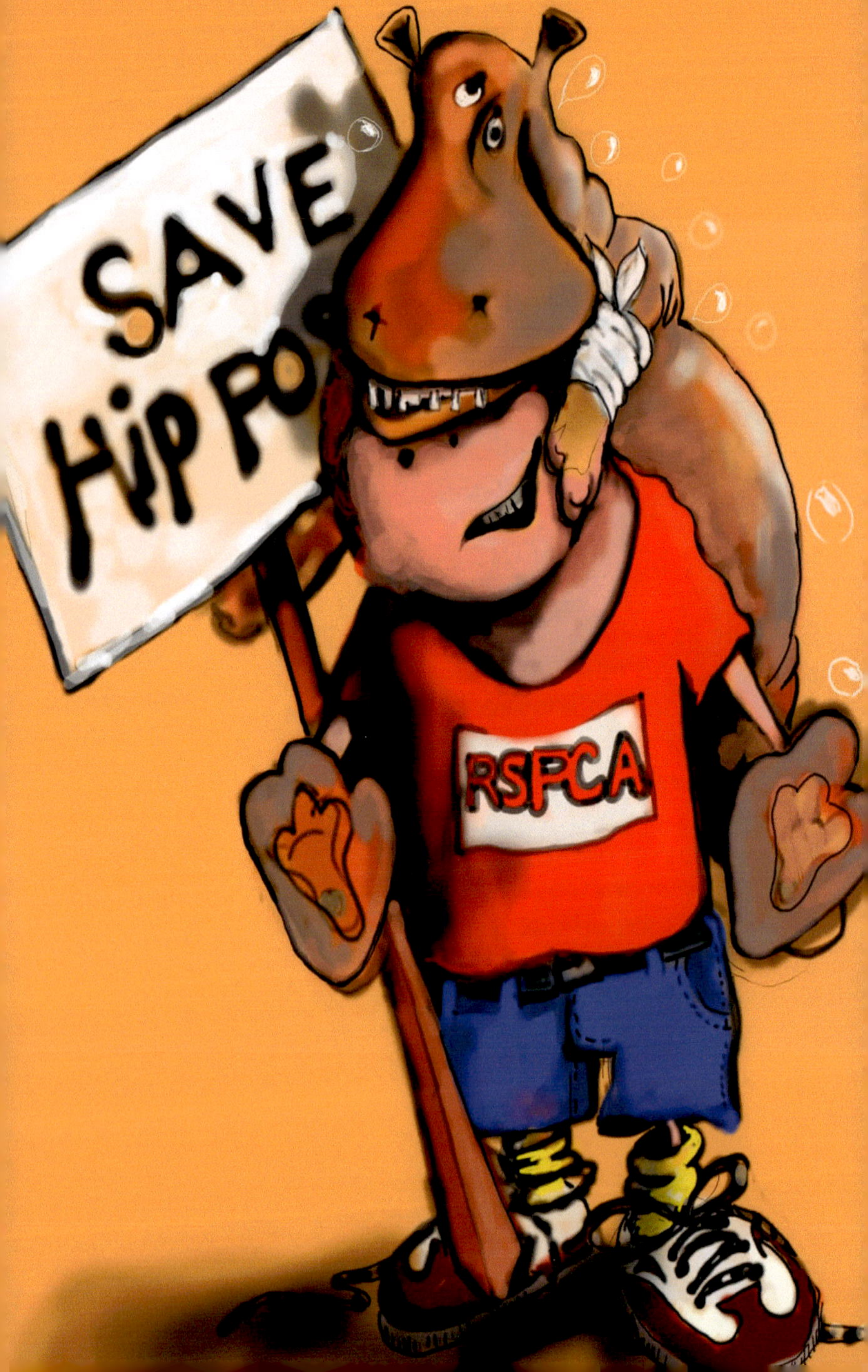
SAVE
HiP PO
RSPCA

Hippo Soup

Did you know the first ever soup was made
from Hippopotamus?
The hungry cavemen back then didn't make much fuss.
They chased poor Mr Hippo all day and all night.
Giving him no sleep and some awful frights.

The cavemen gulped down their hippo soup,
And gave their bowls a good licking.
It was thousands and thousands of years,
Before we made tomato soup and chicken.

But placed on a shelf in a faraway jungle store,
Next to the potatos close to the floor.
You may find a tin of hippo soup still in good condition.
But don't bring it back to London, as the RSPCA
will fight you with a big petition.

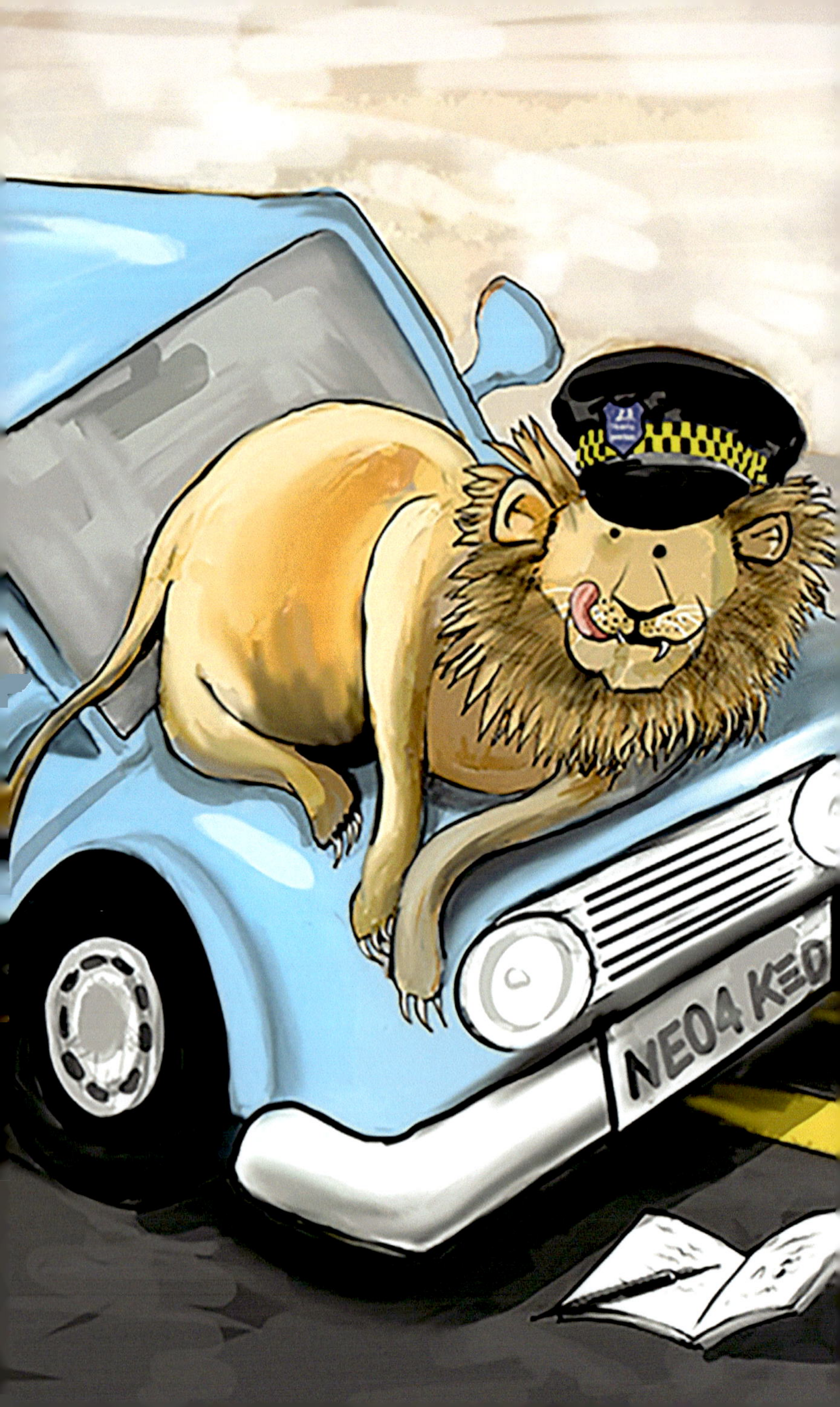
NE04 KED

The Lion and the Traffic Warden

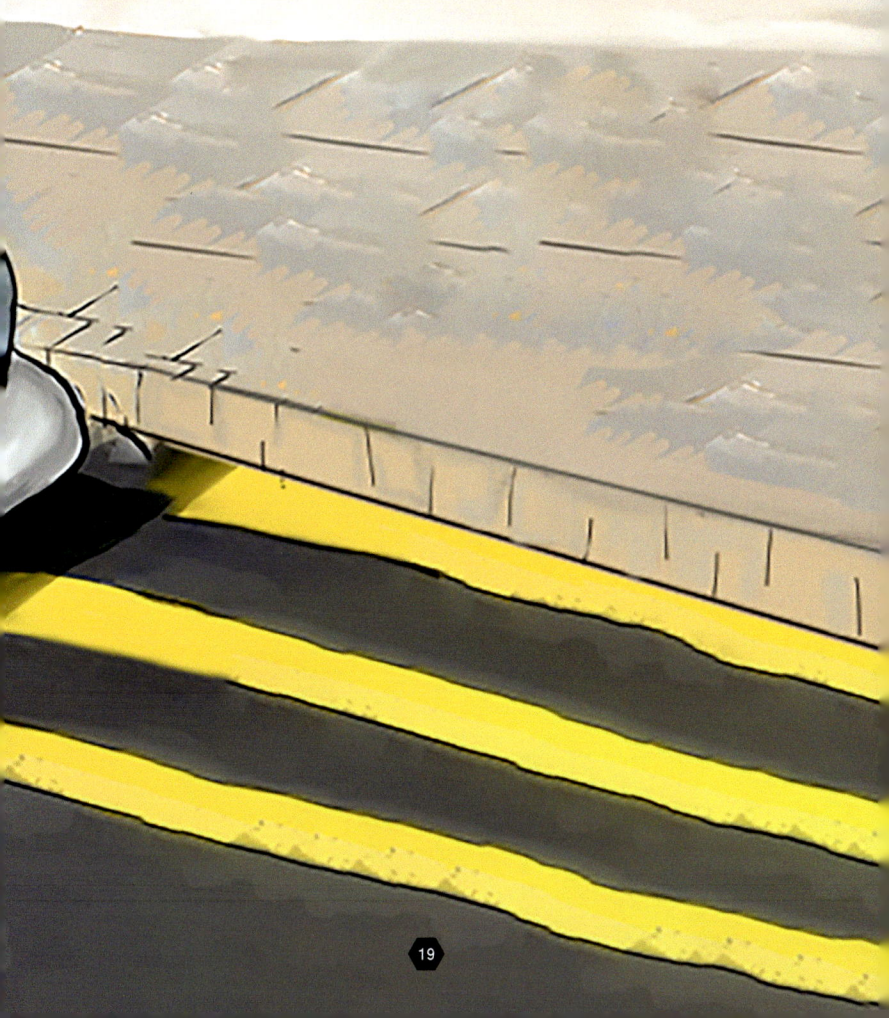

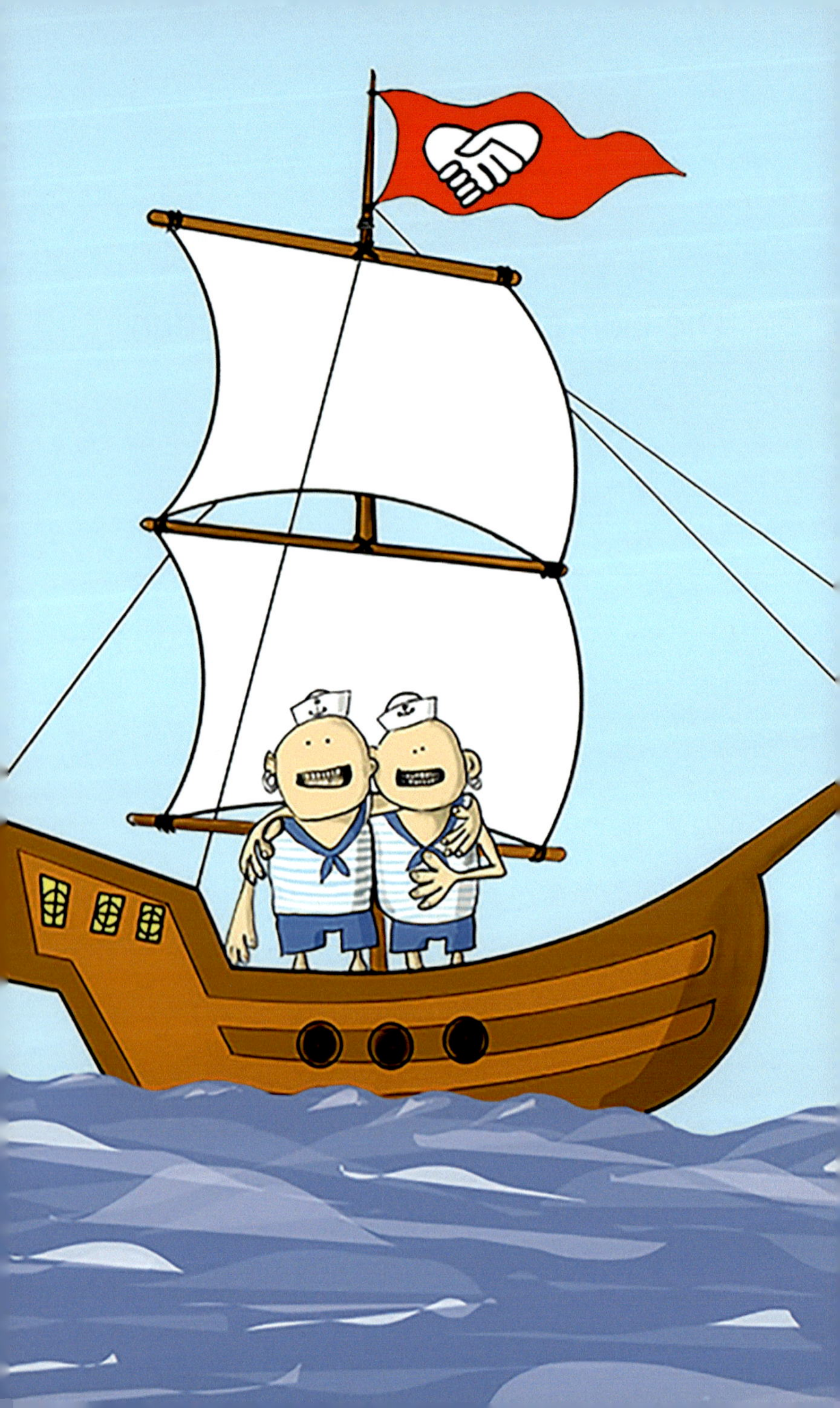

The Best Ship

The little ship is a fine ship that sails true and firm.
The big ship is a bold ship, proud and stern.
The Queen's ship rules the seas with might and bright men.
But the most beautiful ship is your friendship,
Please don't let it ever drift away again.

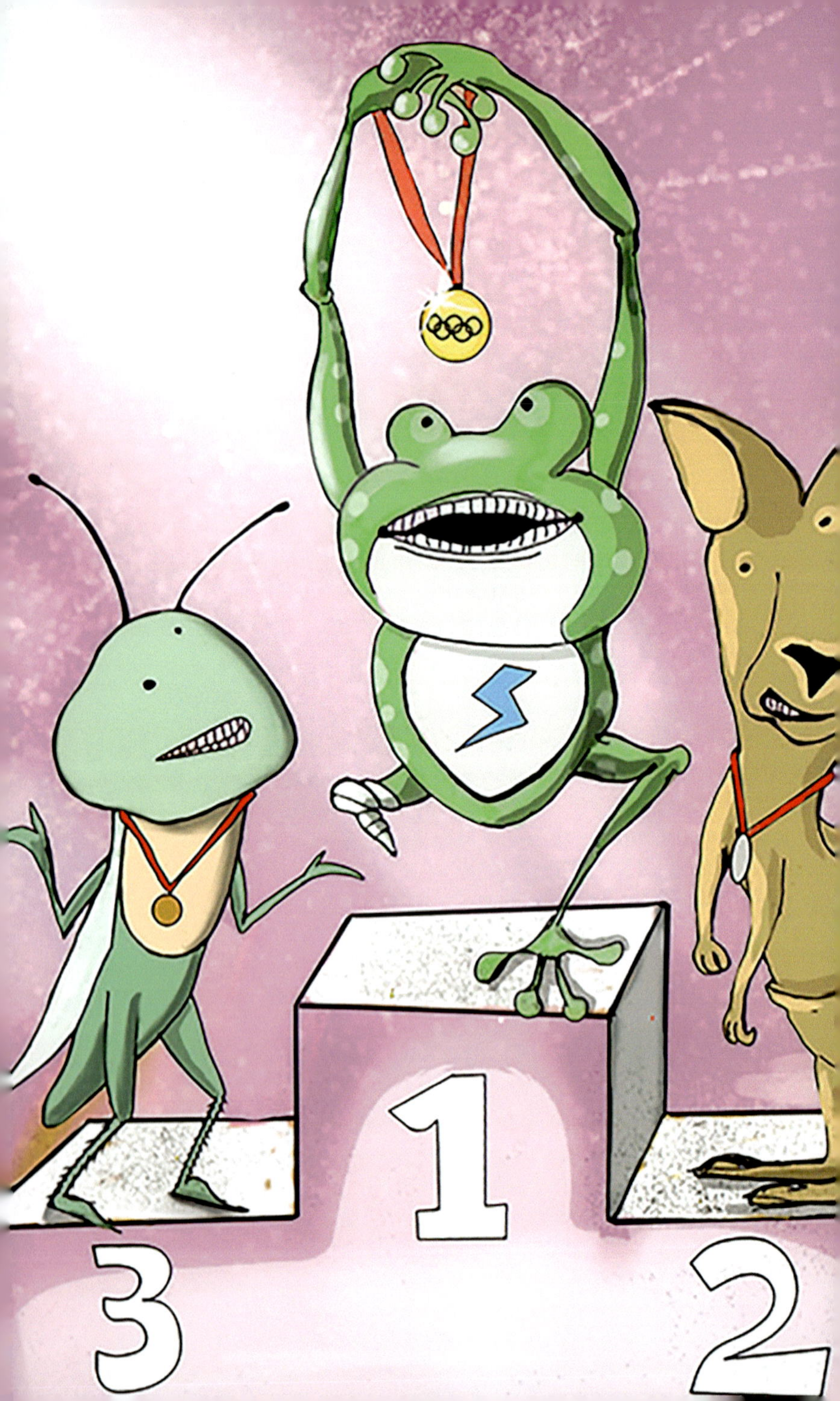
3
1
2

Fredricks the Frog

There was a one-legged frog called Fredericks,
Who stuck his finger in the electrics.
He could never jump very far before,
But now he competes in the Olympics.

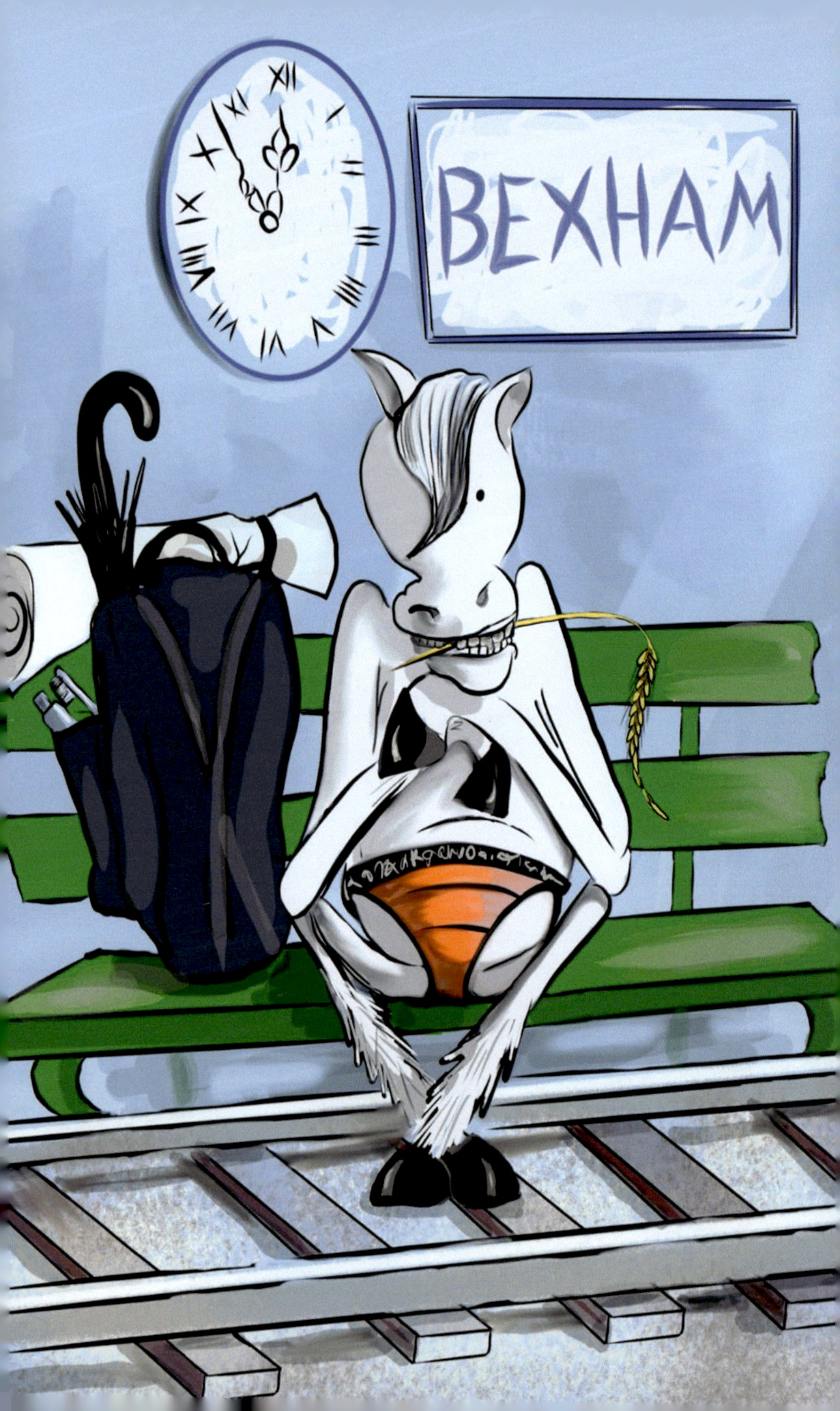
BEXHAM

The Horseham Express

While travelling one day on her majesty's railway,
we stopped at a station called Bexham.
To my surprise a horse was on the platform,
who said he was travelling to Wrexham.

The horse said, 'Neyyyyy, a single please,'
and complained about the time he'd been waiting.
He received his ticket and bounded aboard,
knocking over luggage and all the catering.

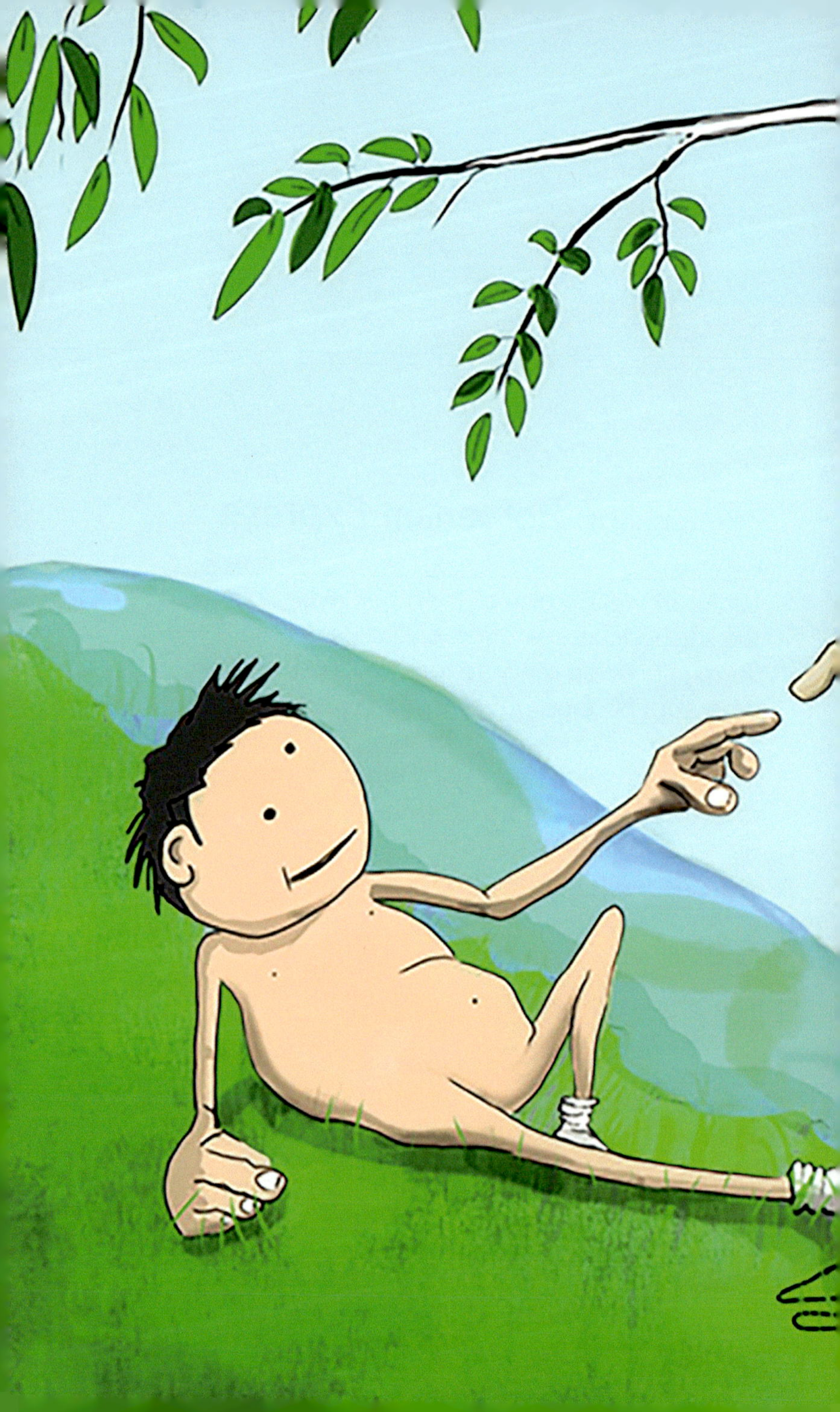

Great Ape

Monkey Monkey swinging through the trees
I wonder if he knows he's related to you and me?

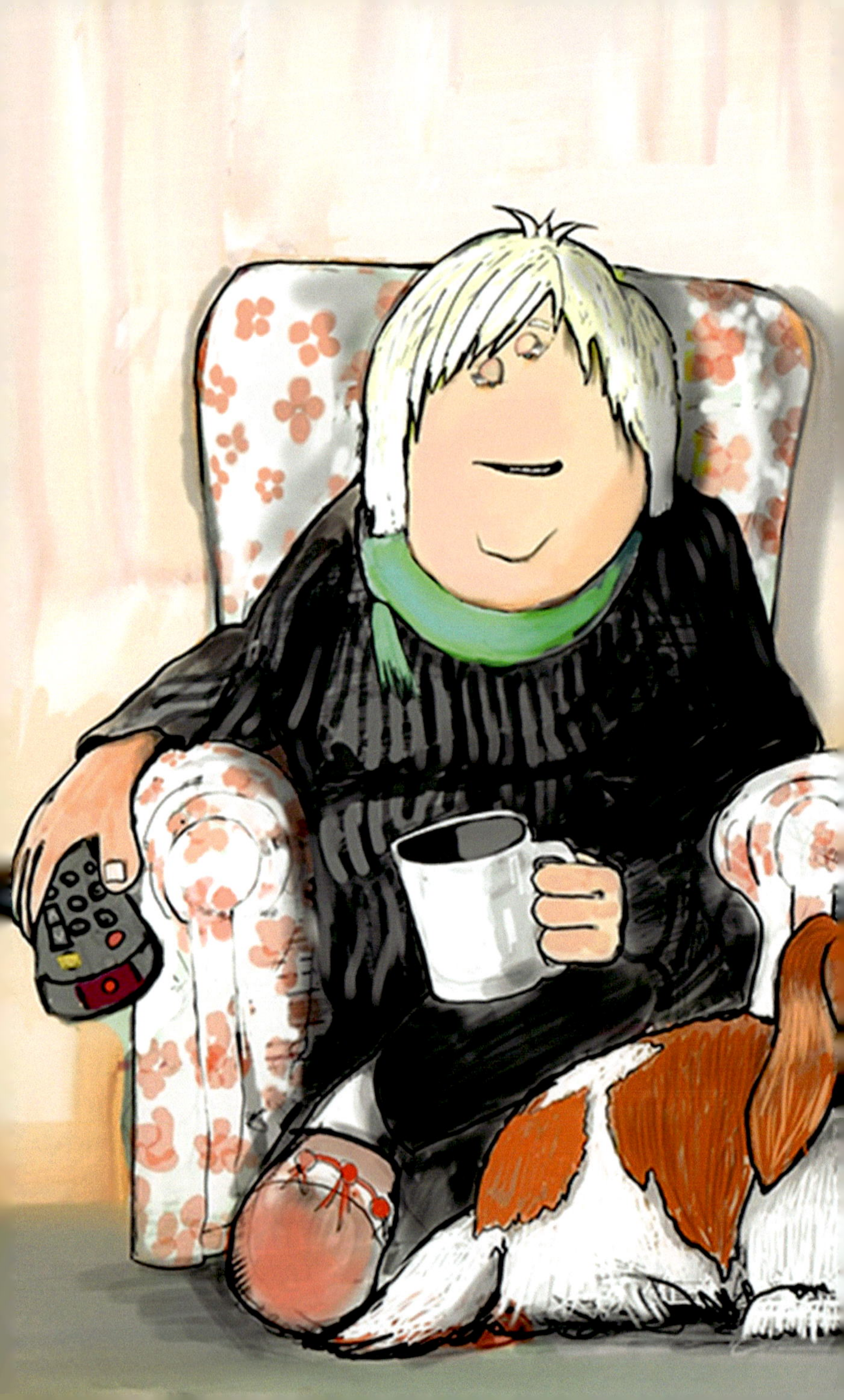

Philbert the Jamaican Flea

Philbert is a big, fluffy Jamaican flea,
he flies around all day long drinking people's tea.

He goes out at night and sips some coconut milk,
and chews on ladies' dresses made from pure silk.

He slurps his favourite rum and wipes his upper lip.
Then jumps on Rover the dog and has a comfy kip.

The Lion and the Naughty Boy!

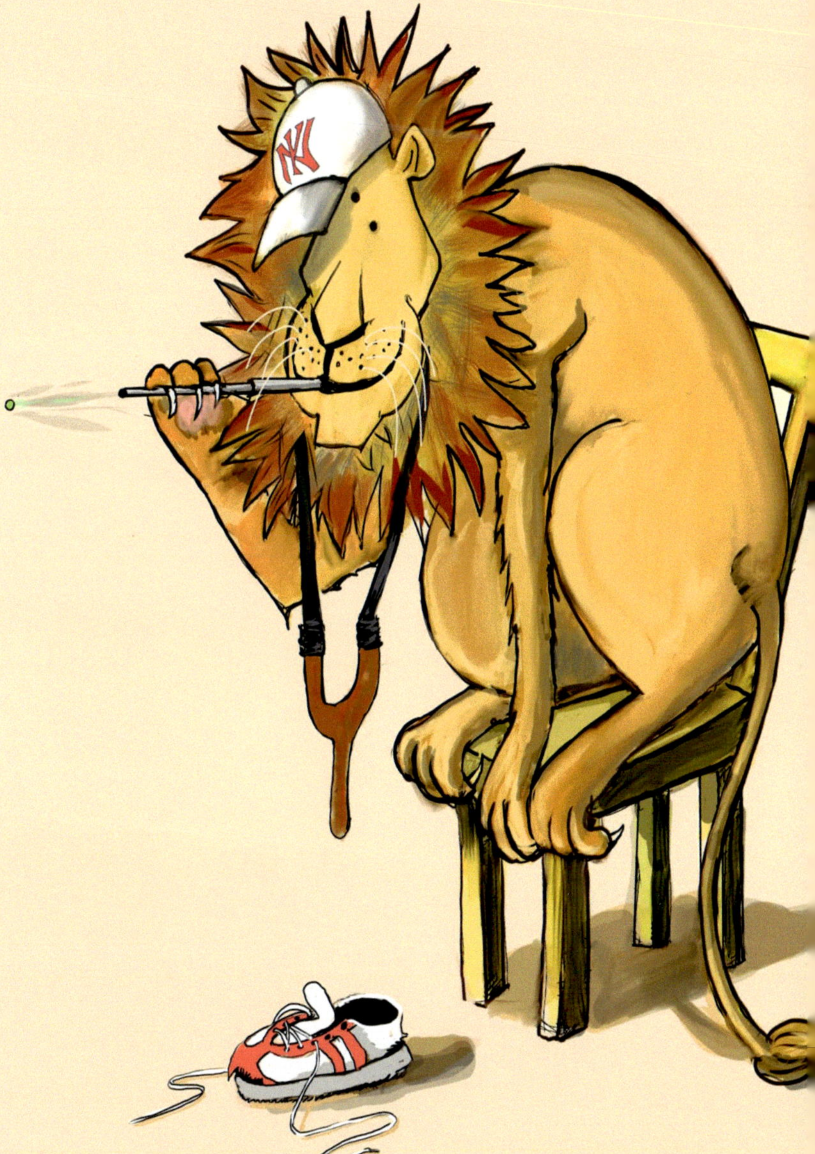

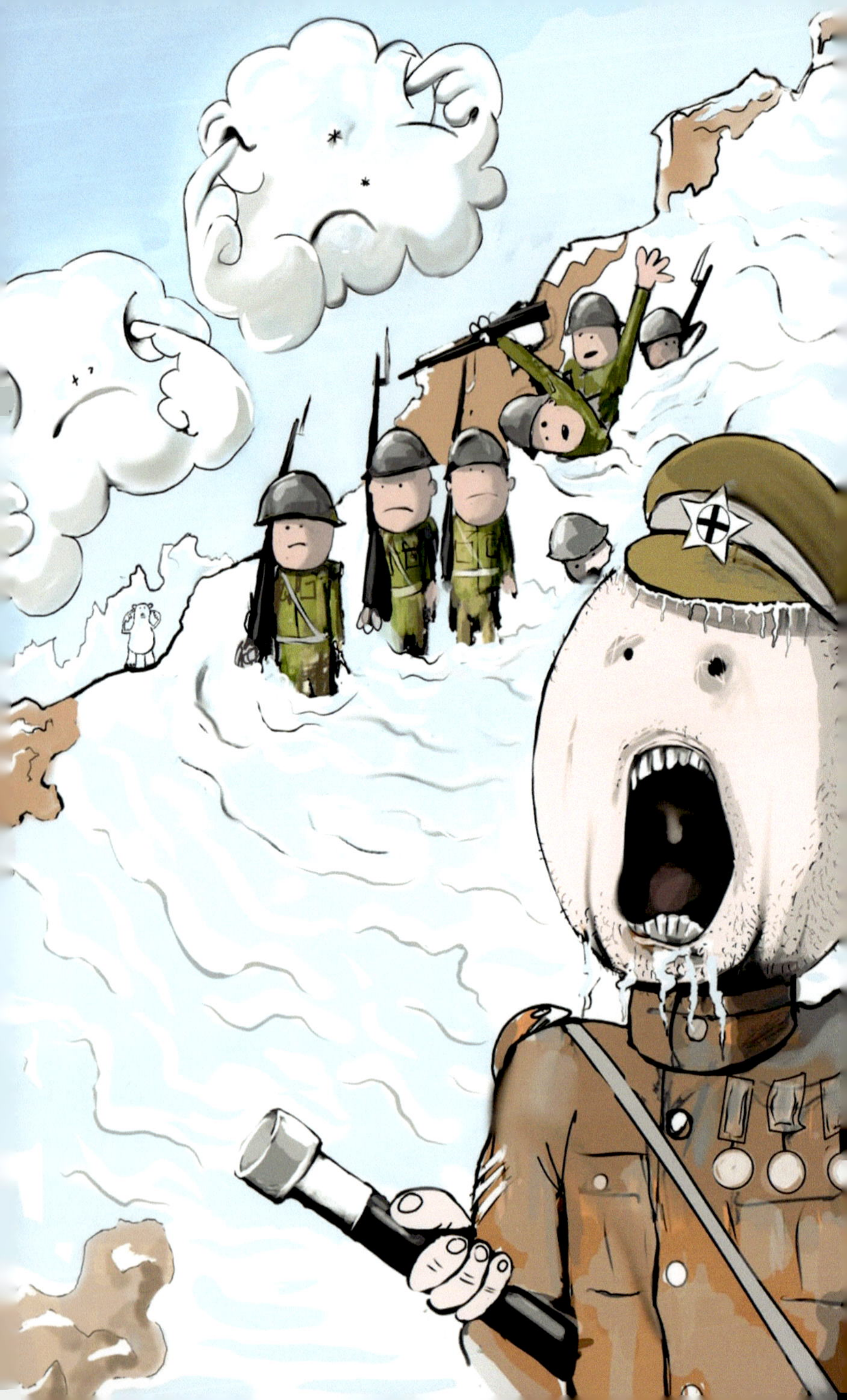

The Sergeant Major

The sergeant major never stopped shouting.
So he was sent to the top of a mountain.
He shouted so loud,
His voice reached the clouds,
And no-one wanted to be around him.

While shouting away on a bleak winter's day,
There was a rumble from deep within.
An avalanche came down
And covered all the ground
Freezing the sergeant's big chin.

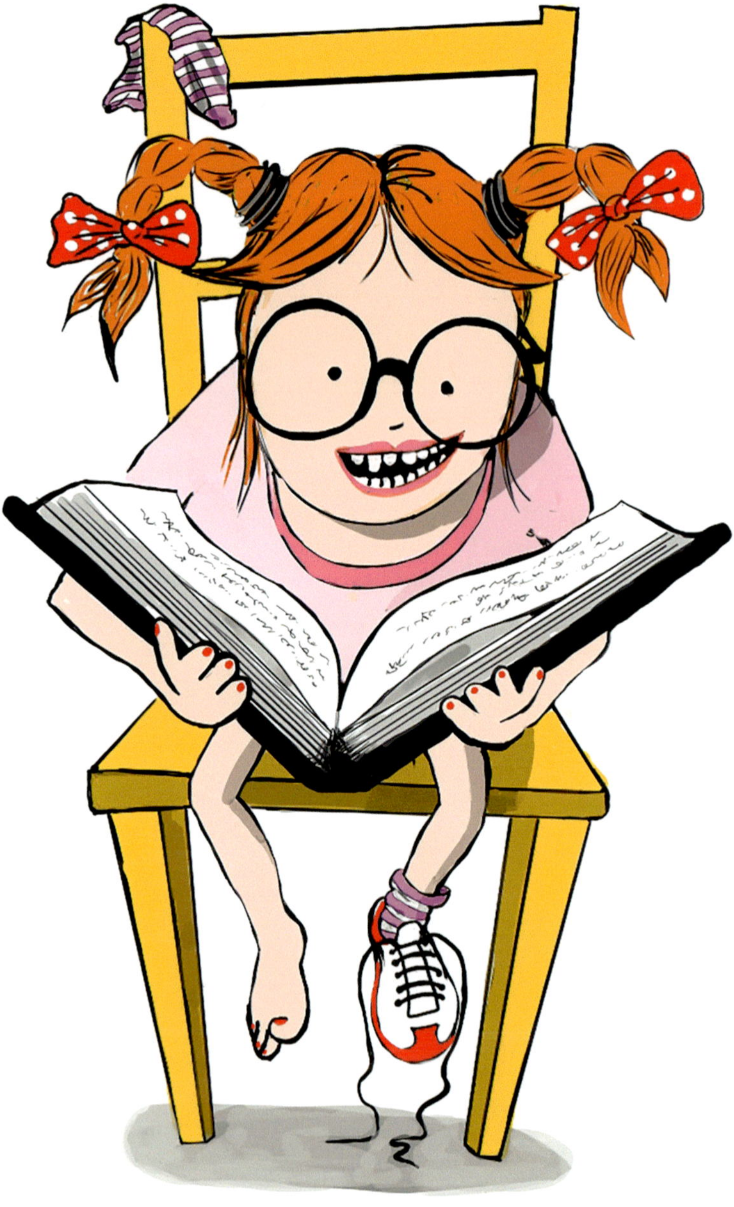

Clever Emma

'It always helps to be clever
whatever the endeavour,'
said Emma,
who was asked to stop studying
for which her reply was... 'No! Never!'
That's why Emma is so clever.

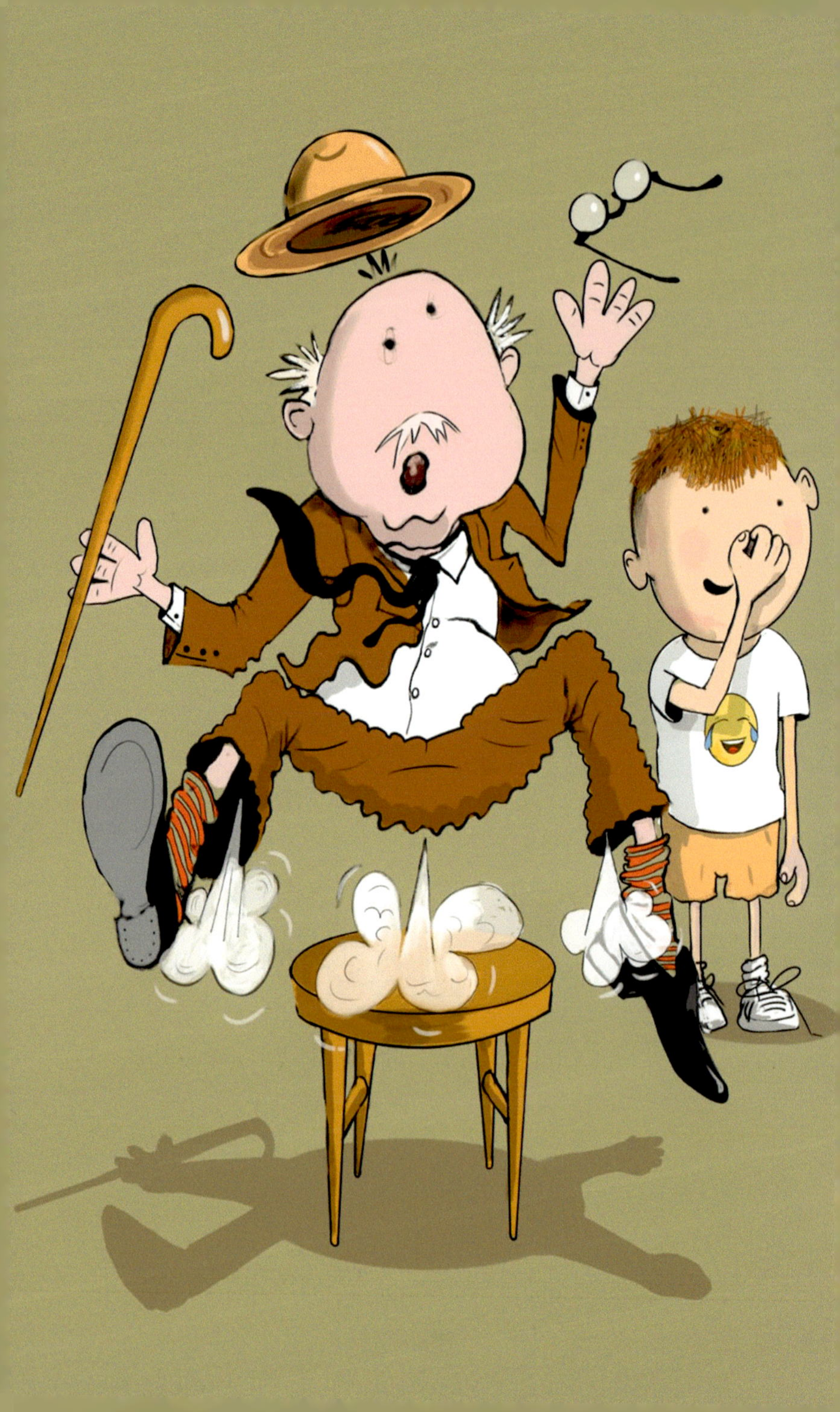

The Great Fart of 2002

On a summer's evening of 2002,
All was peaceful, the sky was blue.
Birds were singing & chirping away,
Everything was well on this very lovely day.

Then all of a sudden, a deep trumpet sound.
Vibrations rose up from the ground.
Grandad began farting and could not be stopped.
The plants around him drooped and flopped.

He gassed and farted for so long,
The people next door could smell the pong.
His teeth did chatter and loosely shake,
His trousers trembled like a mini earthquake.

The windows rattled, the curtains blew,
Please don't give Grandad any more home-made stew.

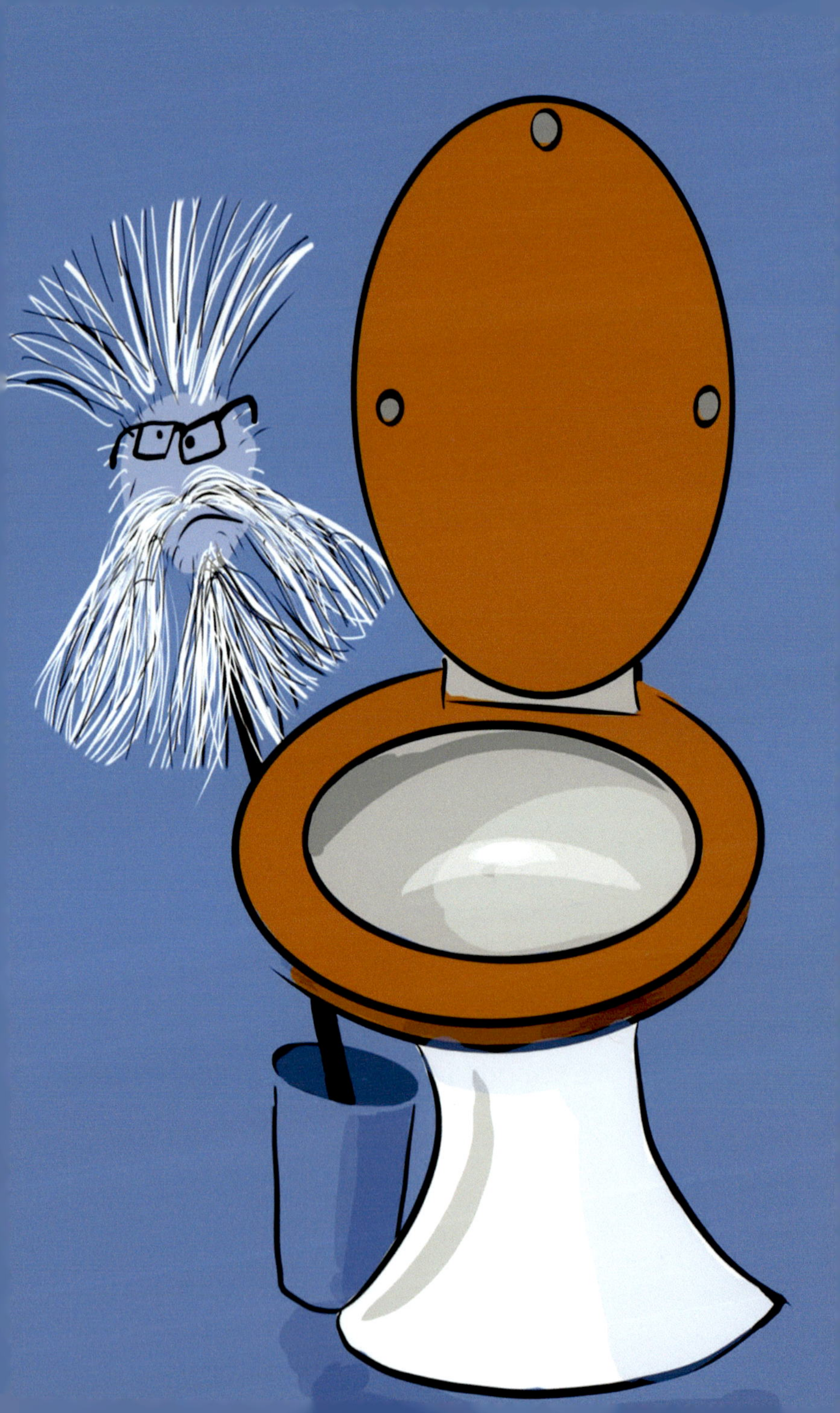

The Toilet Brush

Toilet brush toilet brush
Standing behind the loo.

What an awful life you have
Just waiting to wipe the poo!

Cannibal Values

A full stomach is required for brotherly love and a good deed.
At least that's what the cannibals claimed after a jolly good feed.

Bee Work

Buzzing bee buzzing bee,
Flying around the flowers and trees.
How hard you work dear buzzing bee,
So we can have honey and jam for tea.

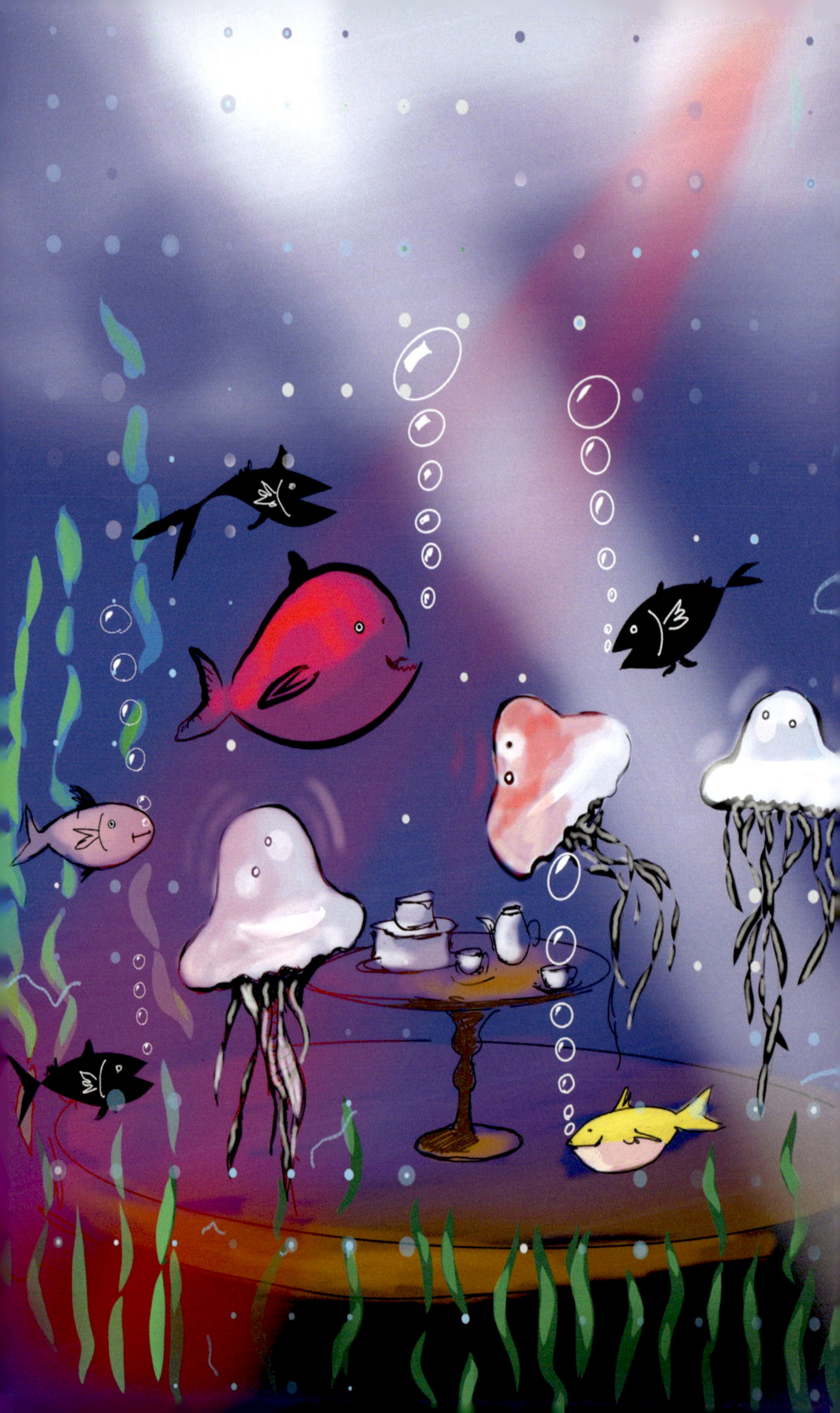

The Jellyfish's Tea Party

While sitting on some rocks looking into the sea,
I see some little tables, chairs and fish laughing...hee hee.
Flashing lights and music play, the guests all dance in huddles.
What are those creatures down below they look like shiny bubbles.

It looked so nice to dive in and join all the fun.
On second thoughts, by the looks of things, I may get badly stung!
You see the things that were dancing all merrily and free,
Were jellyfish eating cake and drinking cups of sea.

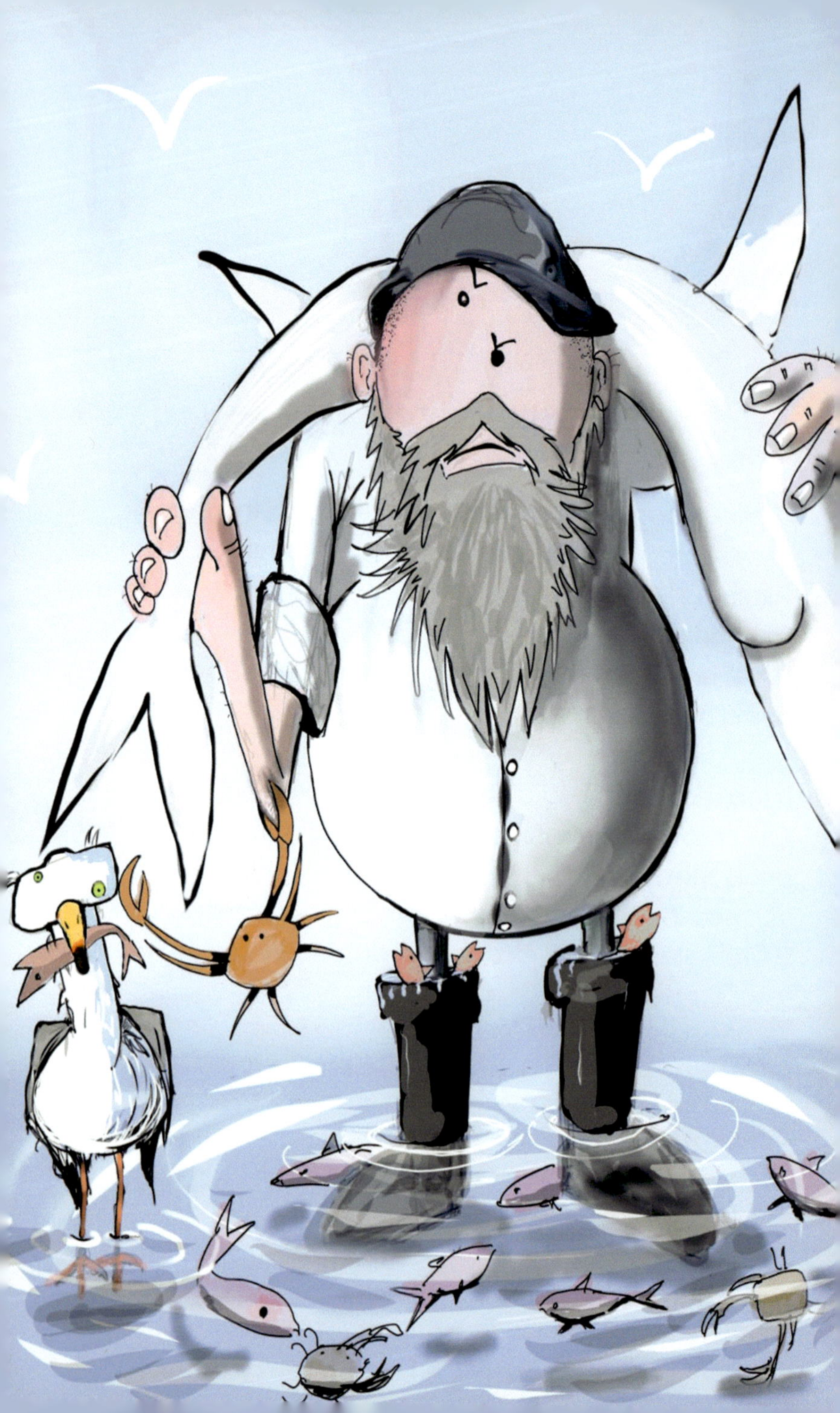

Fisherman Kelly

At the end of the pier sits fisherman Kelly.
He has a long grey beard and a great big belly.
After fishing at sea, he's extremely smelly.
With crabs and fish swimming around in his wellies.

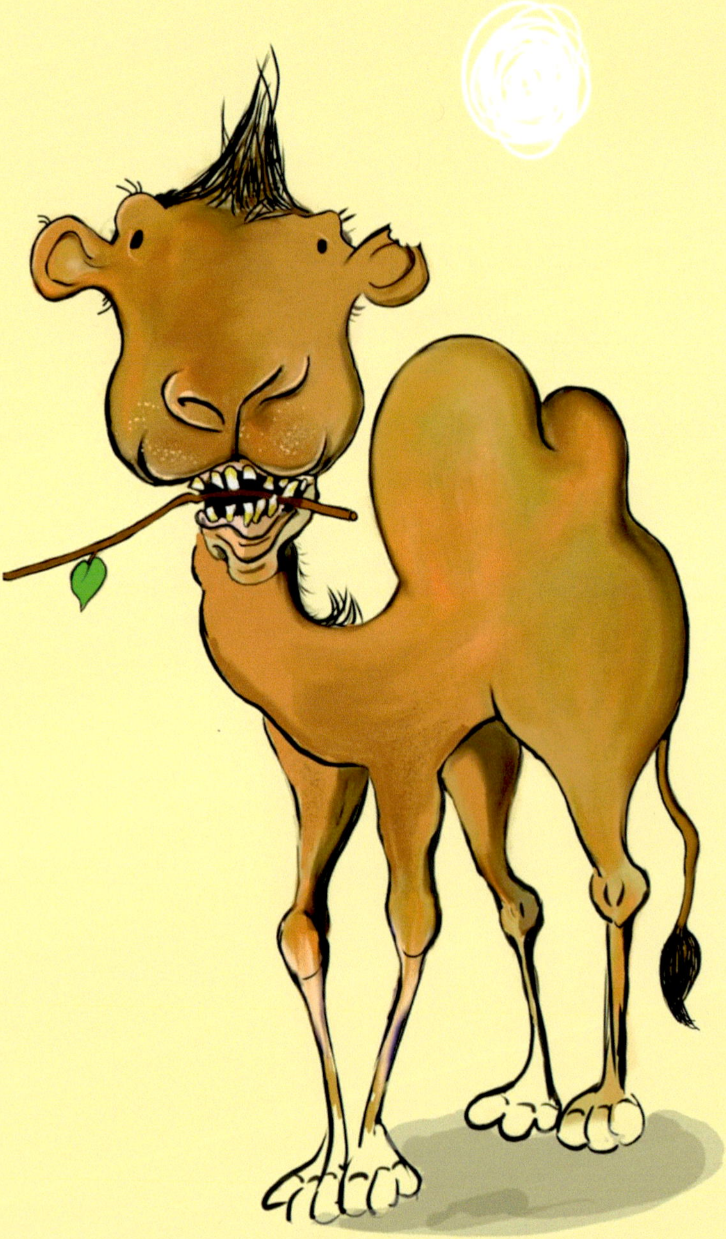

Kevin the Camel

Kevin the camel only eats dry plants and twigs,
And if he's lucky the occasional fig.

One day, he is so hungry he eats a desert shrub.
I bet he'd prefer lunch at my local pub.

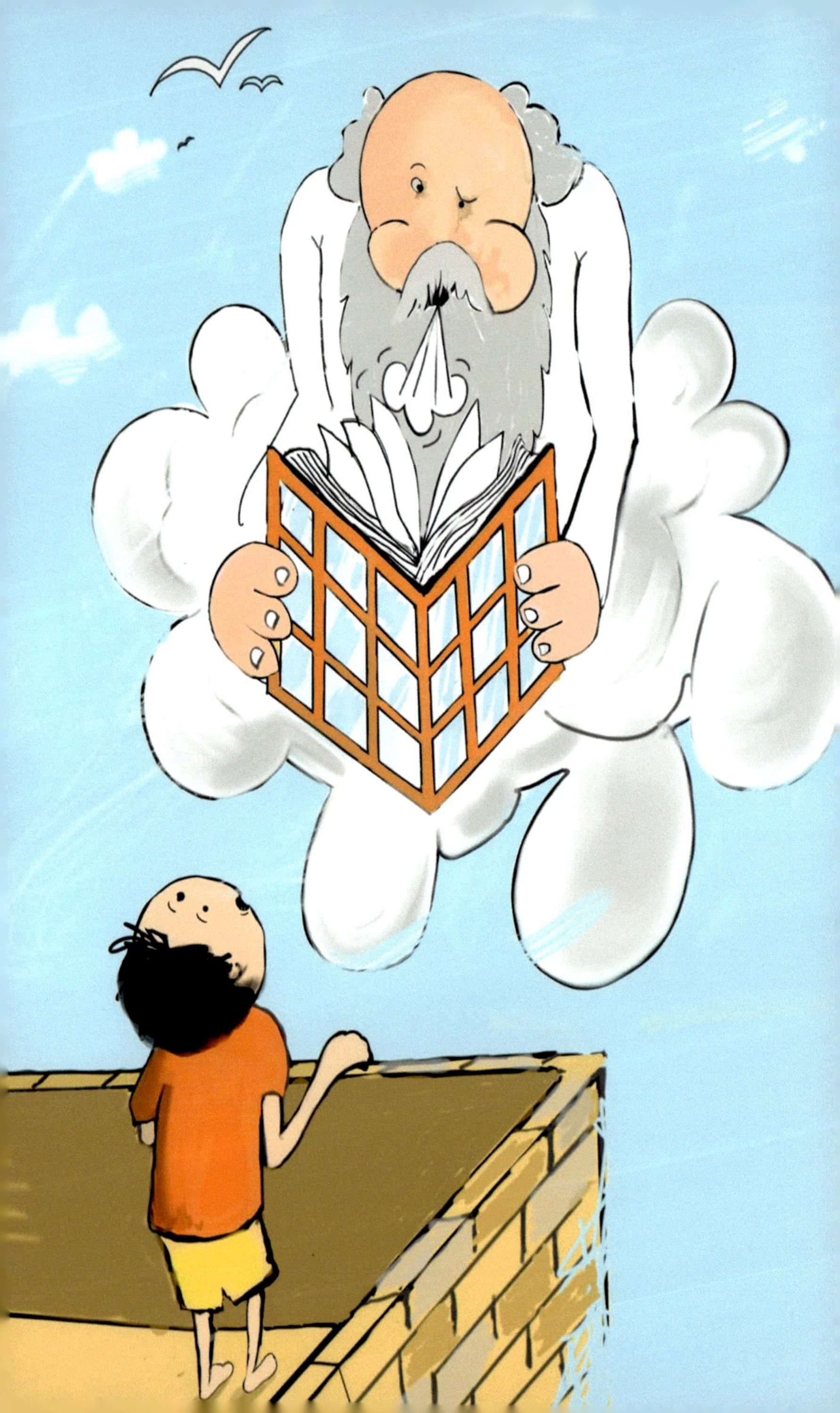

Wind Holes

Did someone leave a window open in heaven?
It's windy down here

And I do fear
That God left it open at about half past seven.

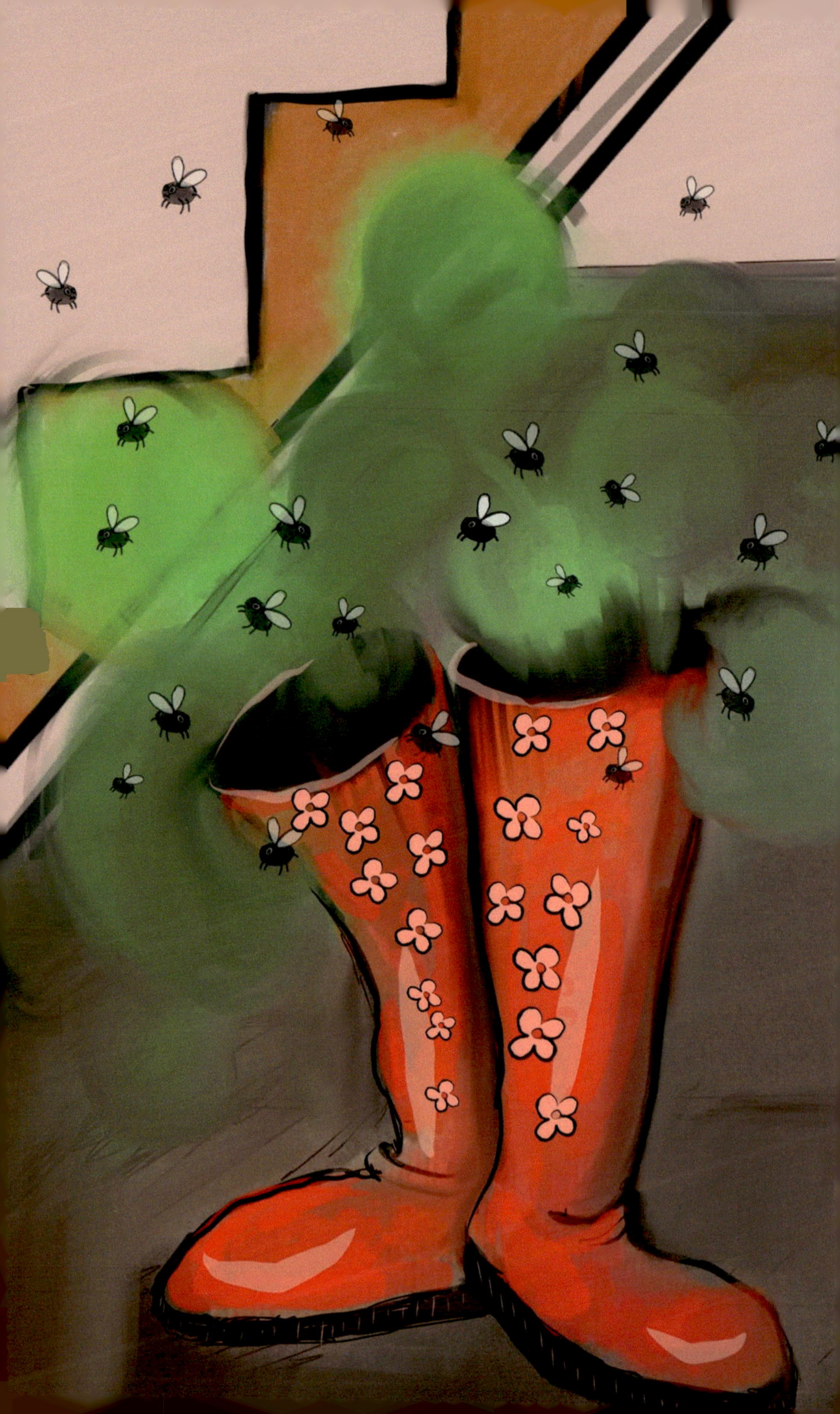

Smelly Wellies

'What is that awful smell?
Where is it coming from, Kate?'
'I don't know, but my eyes are watering,
and the smell is hard to take.'

We look and check all over,
in the cupboards and under the sink.
But still, we cannot find,
that awful, rotten stink.

We wander in the hallway,
the smell is getting stronger.
I hope we find the cause soon,
my nose can't take this any longer.

In the cupboard underneath the stairs
there is an old bag with rising green fog.
Our eyes are watering,
it even distresses Millie, the family dog.

We put pegs on our noses,
and open the bag with a stick at arms-length.
But it's not toxic waste or old rotting fish,
but Mum's smelly wellies were the awful stench.

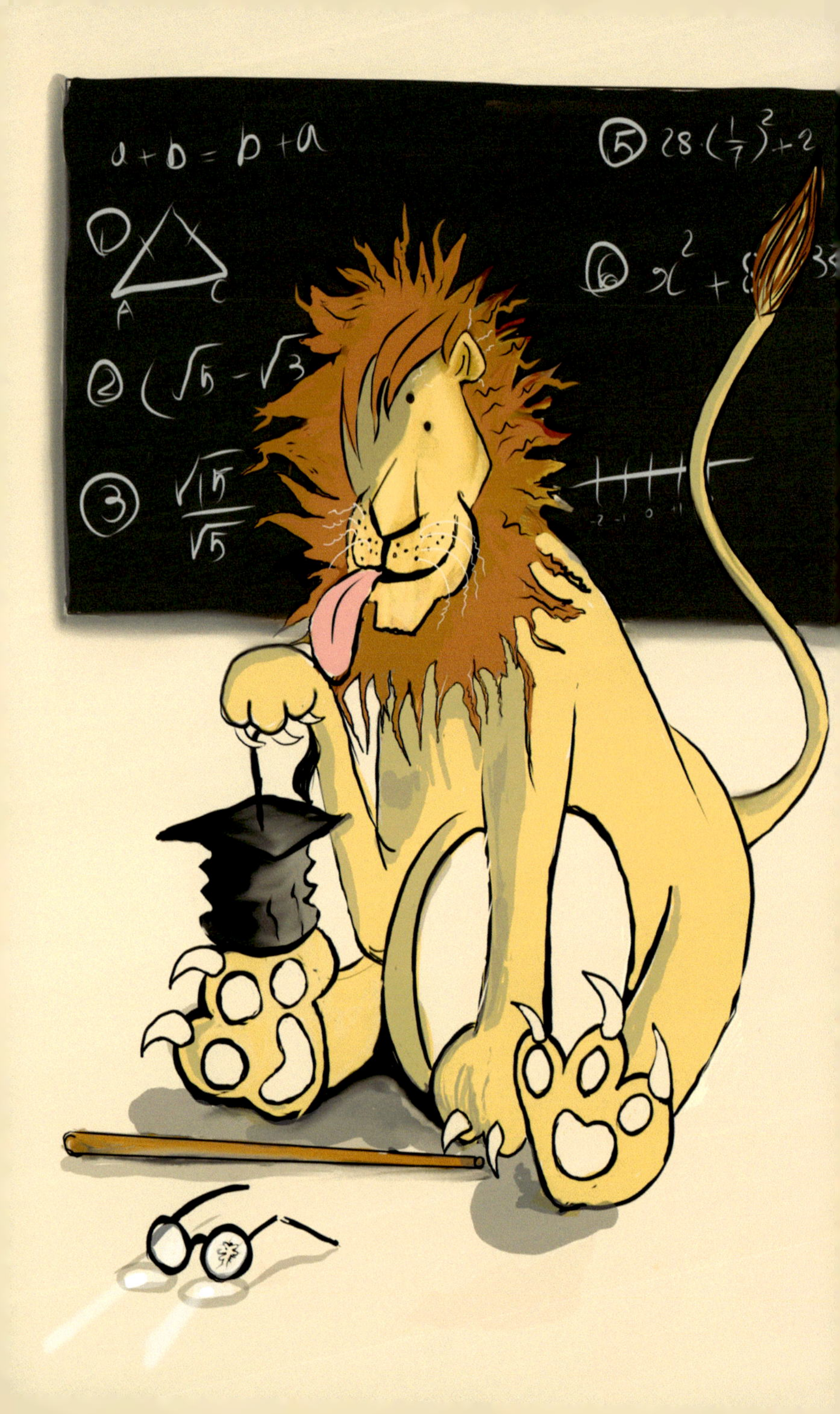

a+b=b+a
A
C

The Lion and the Maths Teacher

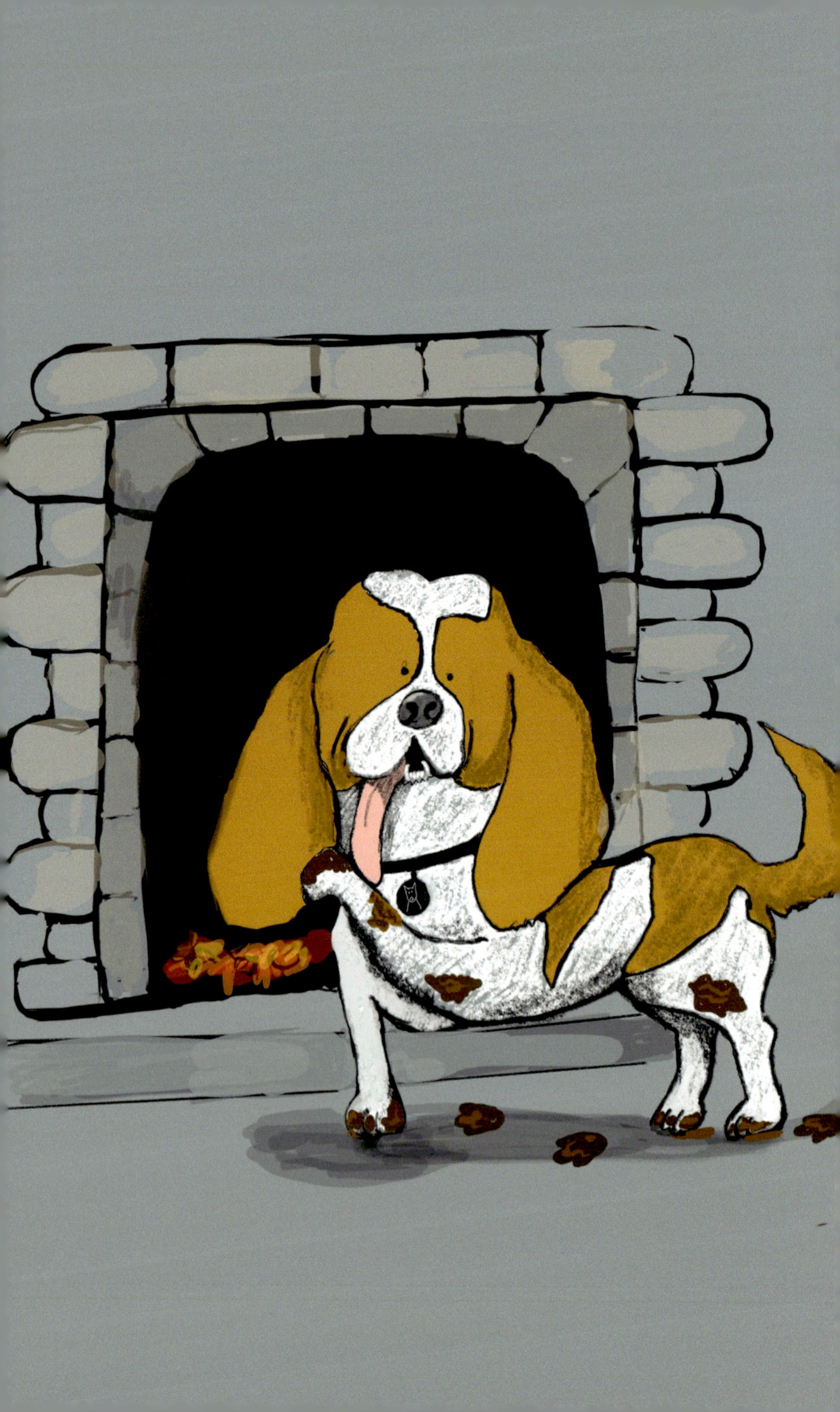

The Pup Sherry

There was a young spaniel called Sherry.
She loved to role in sheep's poo and be smelly.
Sitting in front of the fire at night,
She lick's the poo from her coat with sheer delight.

But later she has a terrible pain in her belly,
Oh, that silly young pup called Sherry!

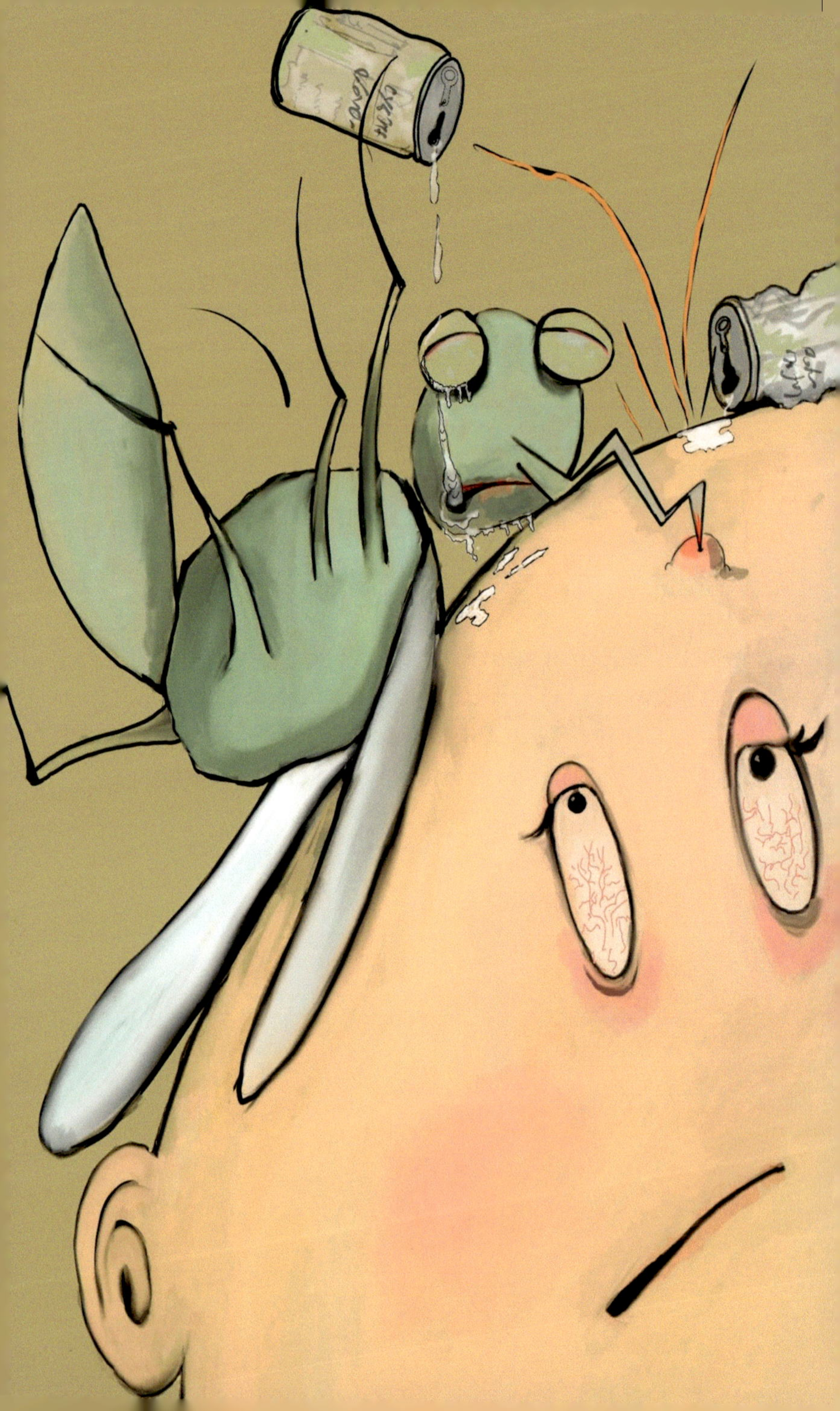

Molly the Mosquito

Buzzzzz, buzzzz, bzzz,
Molly the Mosquito flies around my ear.
She's been up all night laughing and drinking beer.
Swooping down she nibbles dinner from my patterned plate.
Be careful, Molly, you don't want to put on too much weight!

For dessert she'll fly straight up and land upon my head.
Looking for a little drink and perhaps a comfy bed.
She sucks my blood through her tiny nose straw,
Then falls sleep, waking later for a little more.

T.N.T

Fairy Spy Cakes

The secret agent is solving his cases of crime.
He comes across a baddie's website in the nick of time.

He reads the details listed that can make a bomb device,
But instead of closing it down as was his trained advice.

He hatched a plan, to stop the man posting wide and free.
And changed the bomb ingredients with a sticky bun recipe for tea.

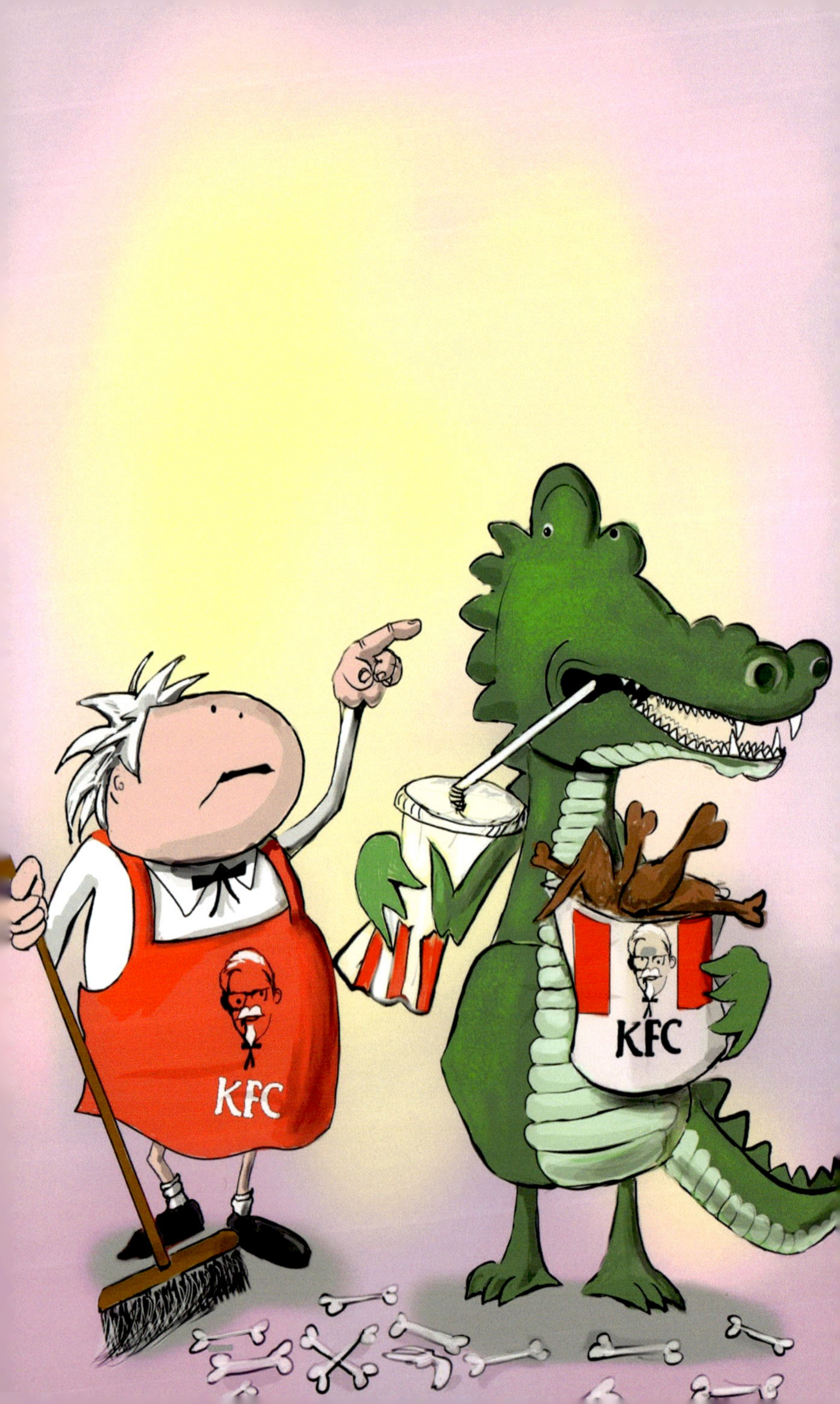
KFC
KFC

Colin the Crocodile

Colin the crocodile munches on some meat.
He chews arms, legs and sometimes even feet.

Swimming and eating are Colin's favourite things,
And going to KFC for some barbecued chicken wings.

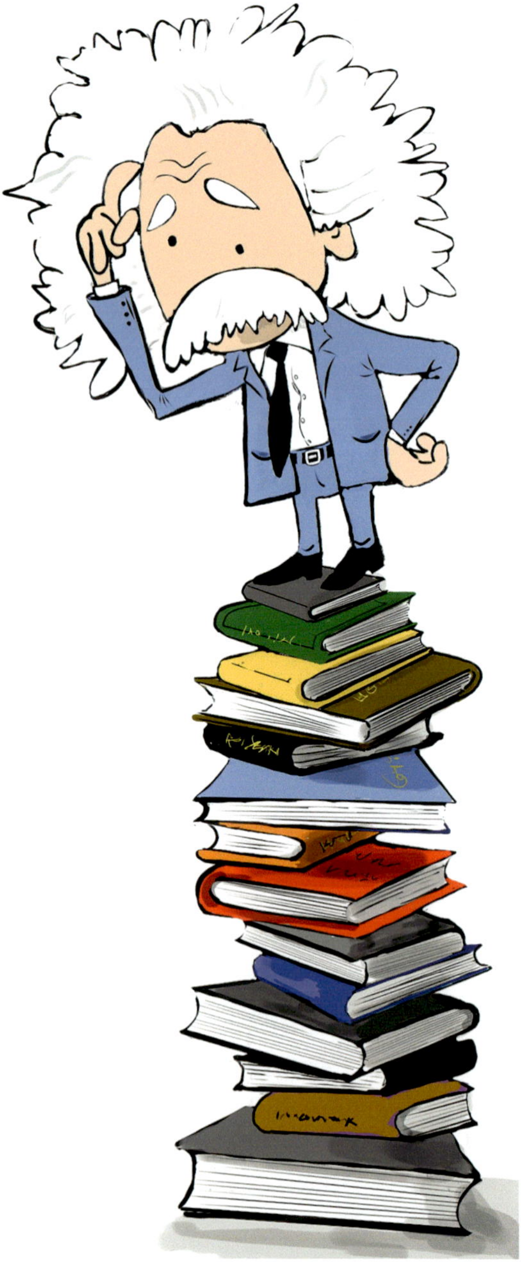

The Worried Professor

The professor is worrying and trying to think.
'All of my new inventions absolutely stink!
When did I last have a good idea?' he sobs,
as he shines the brass of his handsome doorknob.

It's been quite some time,
since I last defined
the mere notion of any idea at all!

I'm bright and I'm clever,
but I can't be a professor
with no good inventions at all.

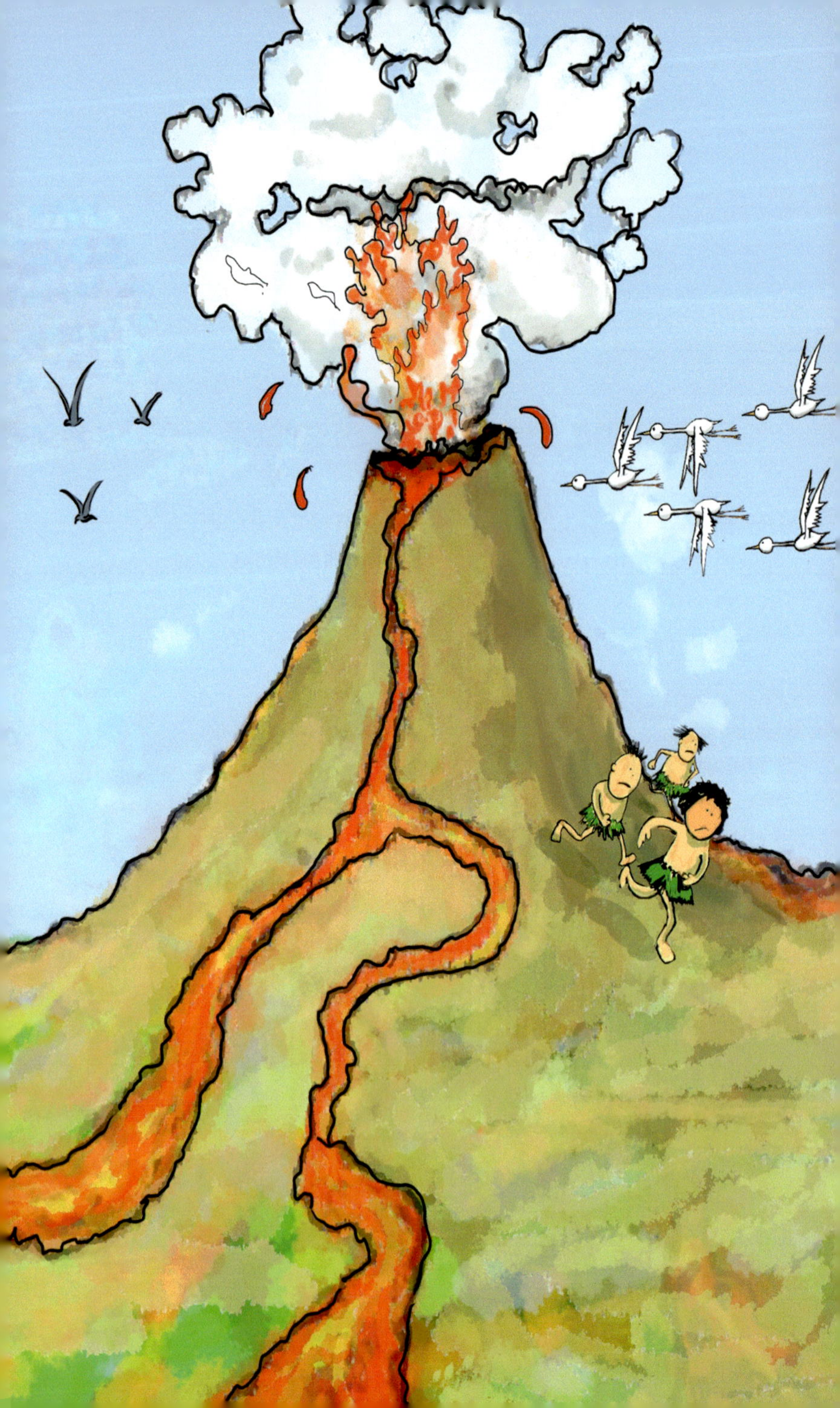

Volcano

A volcano is a mountain of re-creation and life.
The flowing red rivers flow steady and rife.

Glowing brightly, spitting hot ash, sliding down rubble.
Later cooling and keeping us above sea level.

So don't fear our world's fire spitting mountains.
And pray they never stop spewing their beautiful
red fountains.

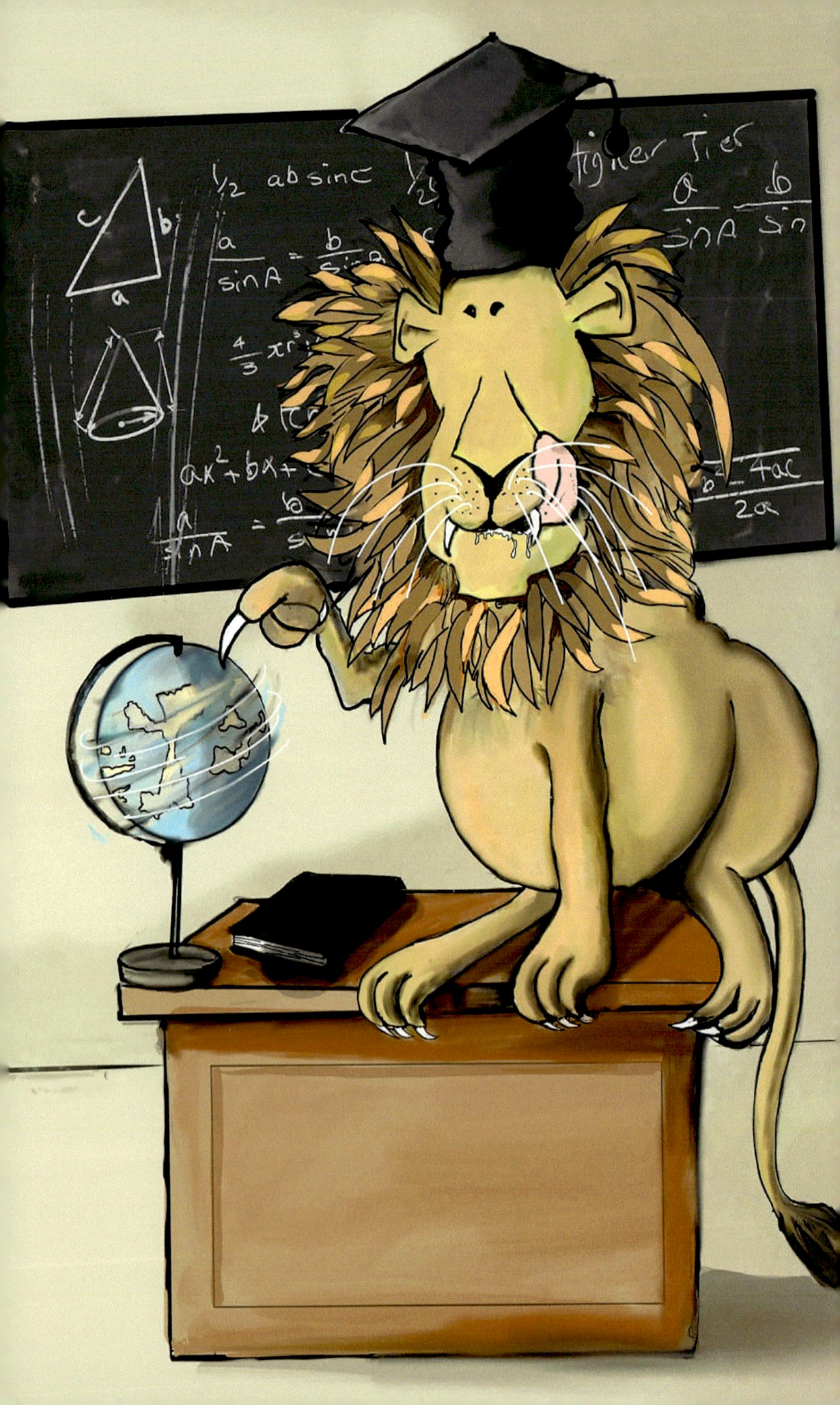
½ ab sinc
tiger Tier

The Lion and the Geography teacher

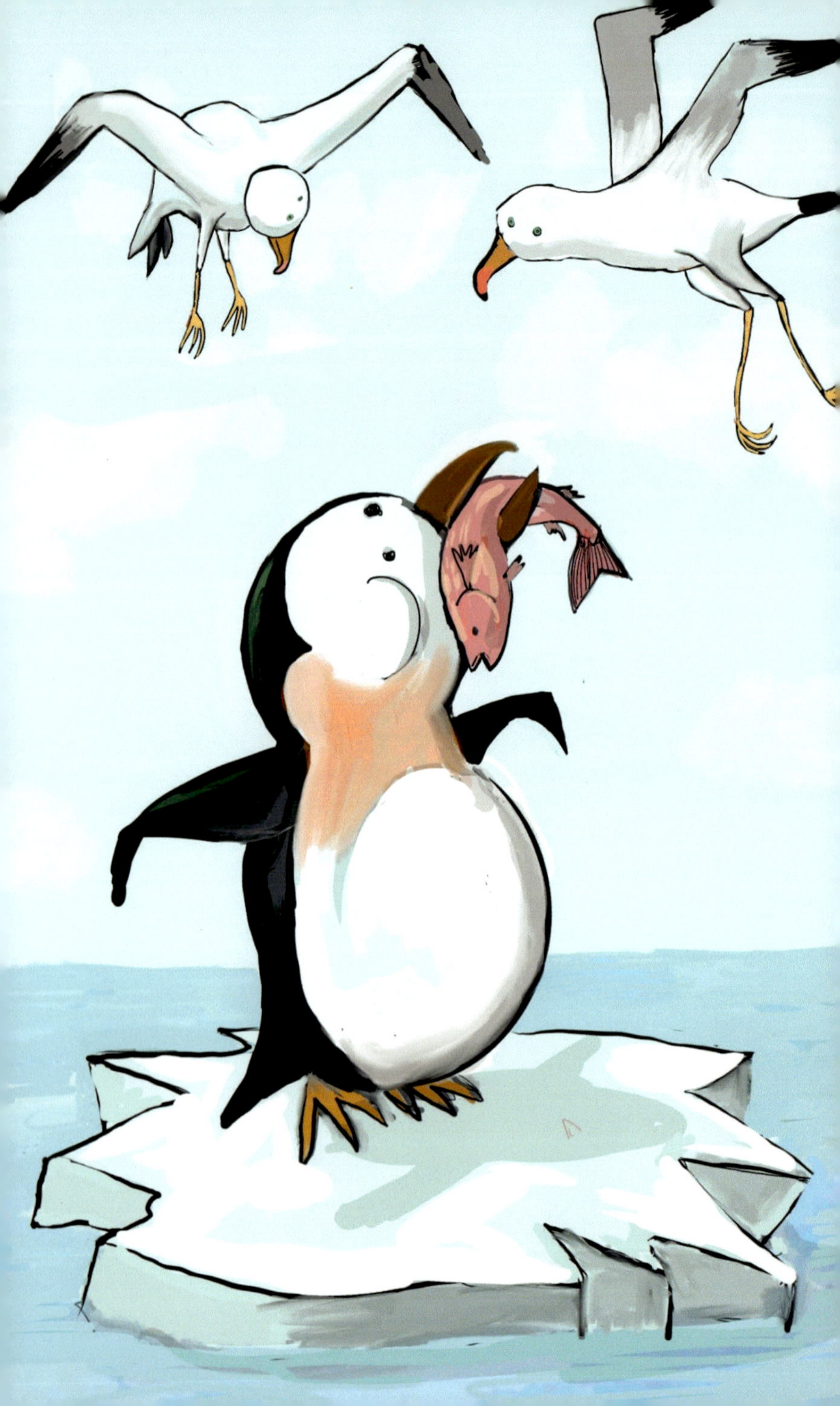

Percy the Penguin

Percy the penguin swims in the sea,
Jumping out on the rocks to munch his fish tea.

He looks up at the birds gliding in the sky,
And wonders why he can't swoop and gracefully fly.

But the birds above look down at Percy jealous with envy,
And wish they could swim deep and fast to catch fish a plenty.

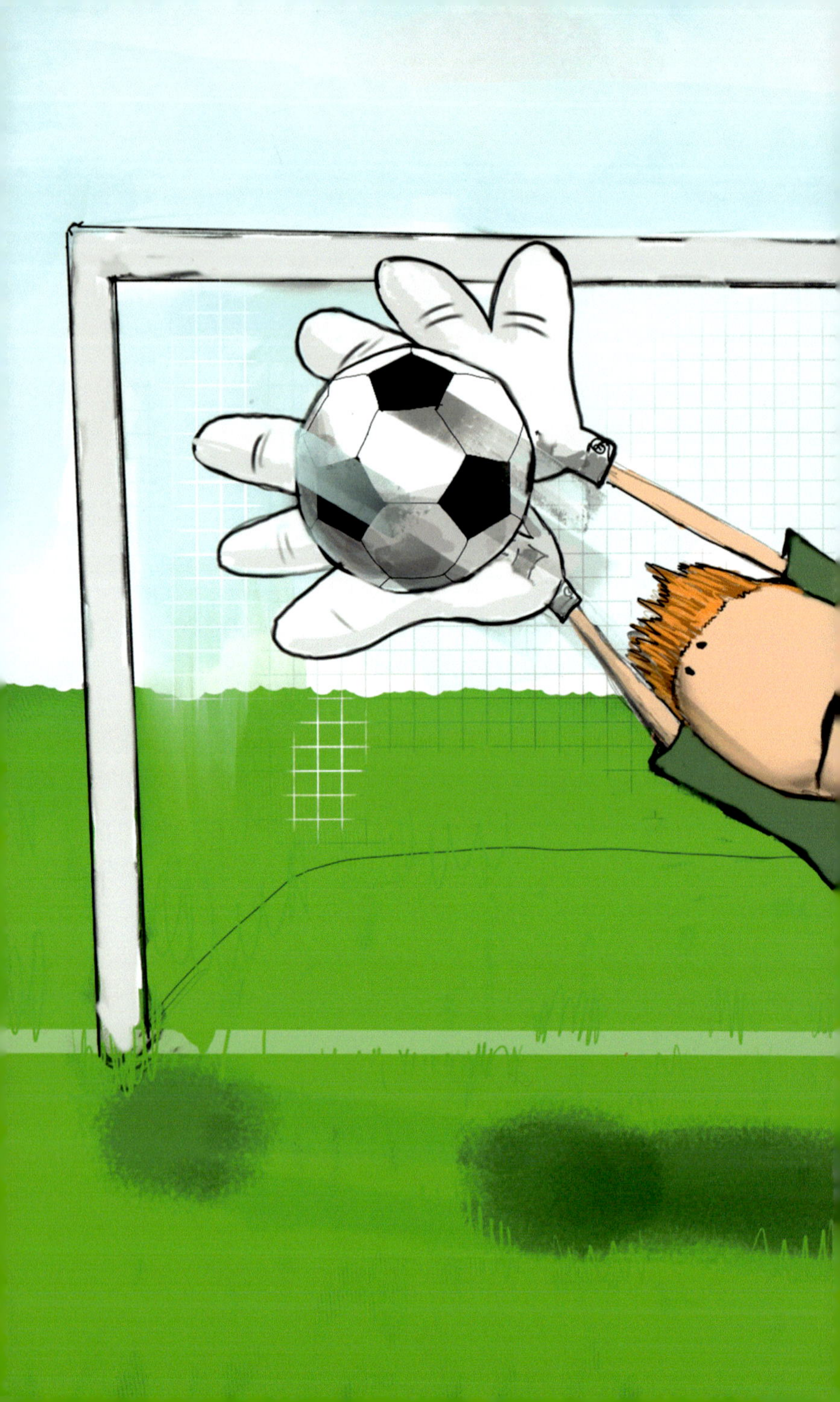

Dave the Goalkeeper

A goalkeeper with huge hands called Dave,
Jumps and dives and is extremely brave.

He wins the cup with an amazing save,
'We love you, Dave!' the crowd cheers and waves.

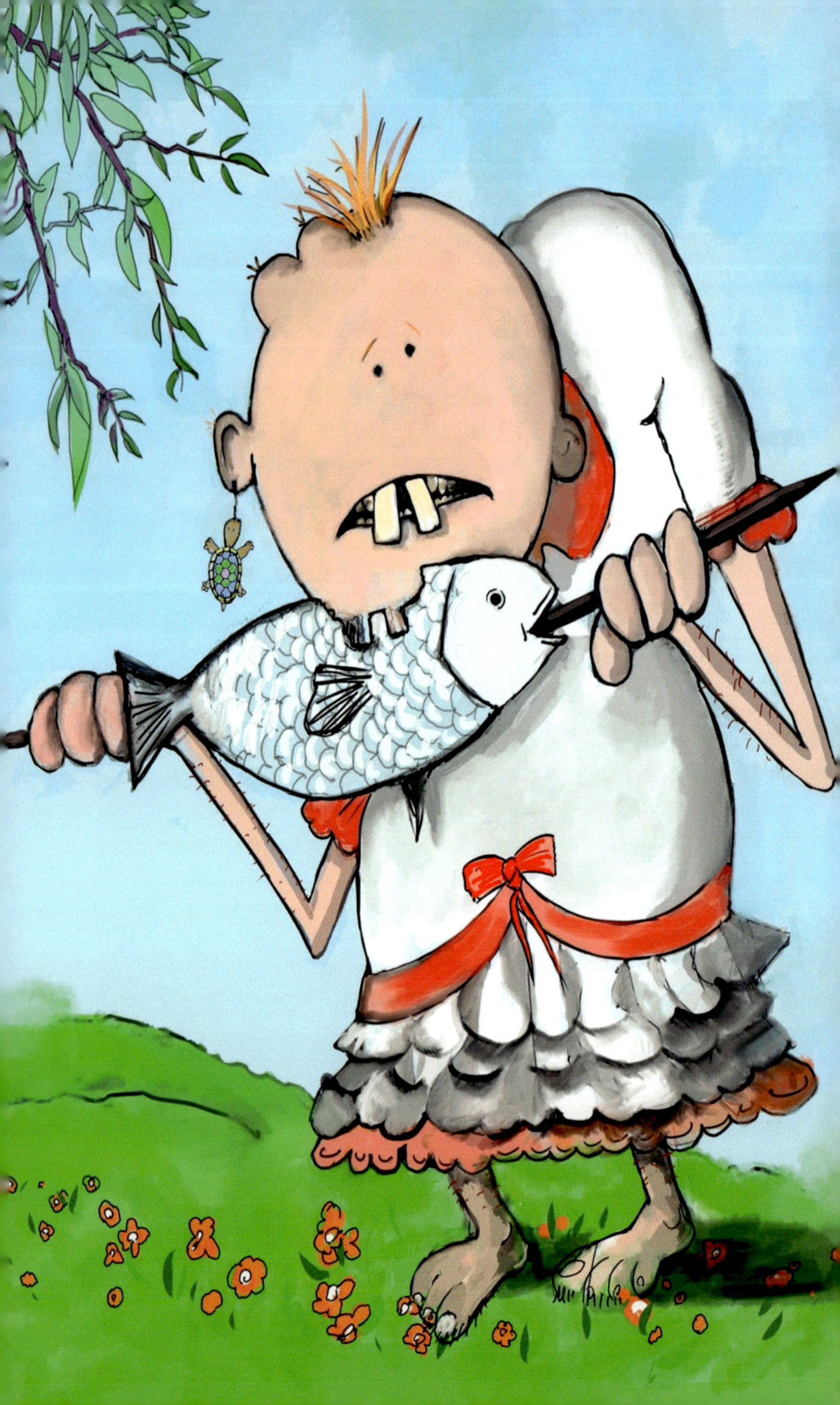

Hubert Humperbump

Hubert Humperbump runs through the hills,
He only wears silk blouses and skirts with big frills.
He has a lumpy back and two bumps on his head,
And likes a cup of warm gravy before he goes to bed.

He has two big teeth sticking out of his mouth,
And no matter where he is they're always pointing south.
Hubert is a friendly boy, but people think him odd,
Apart from his best friend, he's called farmer Todd.

He fishes for his dinner; his favourite is smoked haddock.
He dances round the flowers which are mostly in the paddock.
If you see Hubert while out playing one summer's day,
Ask him if he'll show you his hide out, it's down by Pirates-bay.

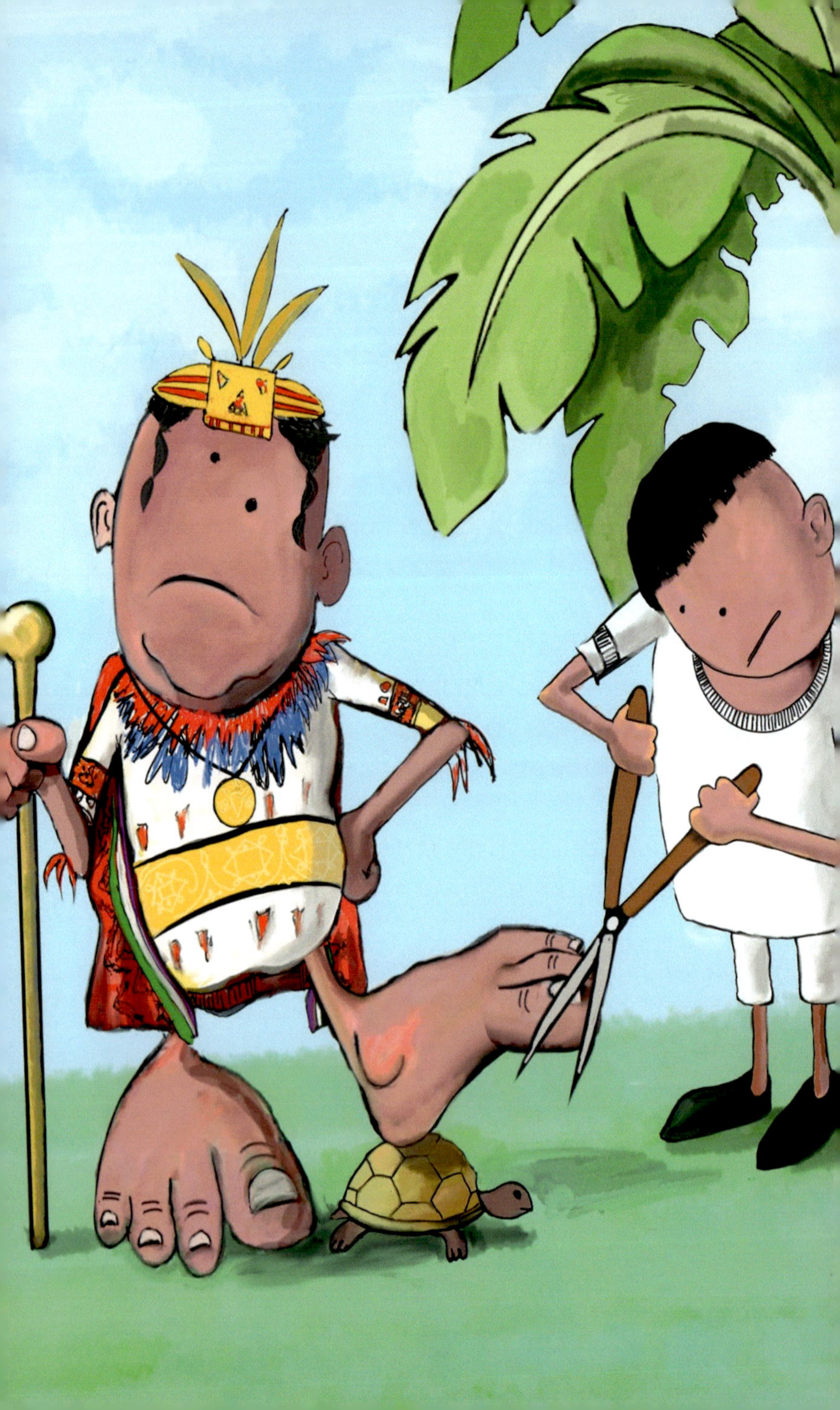

The Prince with Big Feet

Prince Percival of Peru has big feet.
They look like two great slabs of meat.
He falls downstairs and up them too,
They poke out under the door when he's on the loo.

His butler cuts his toenails with the largest garden sheers,
But people still stand on them which reduces him
to tears.
He dances with the princess and kicks her in the shins.
But when he's swimming, he is always first as his big
feet act like fishes' fins.

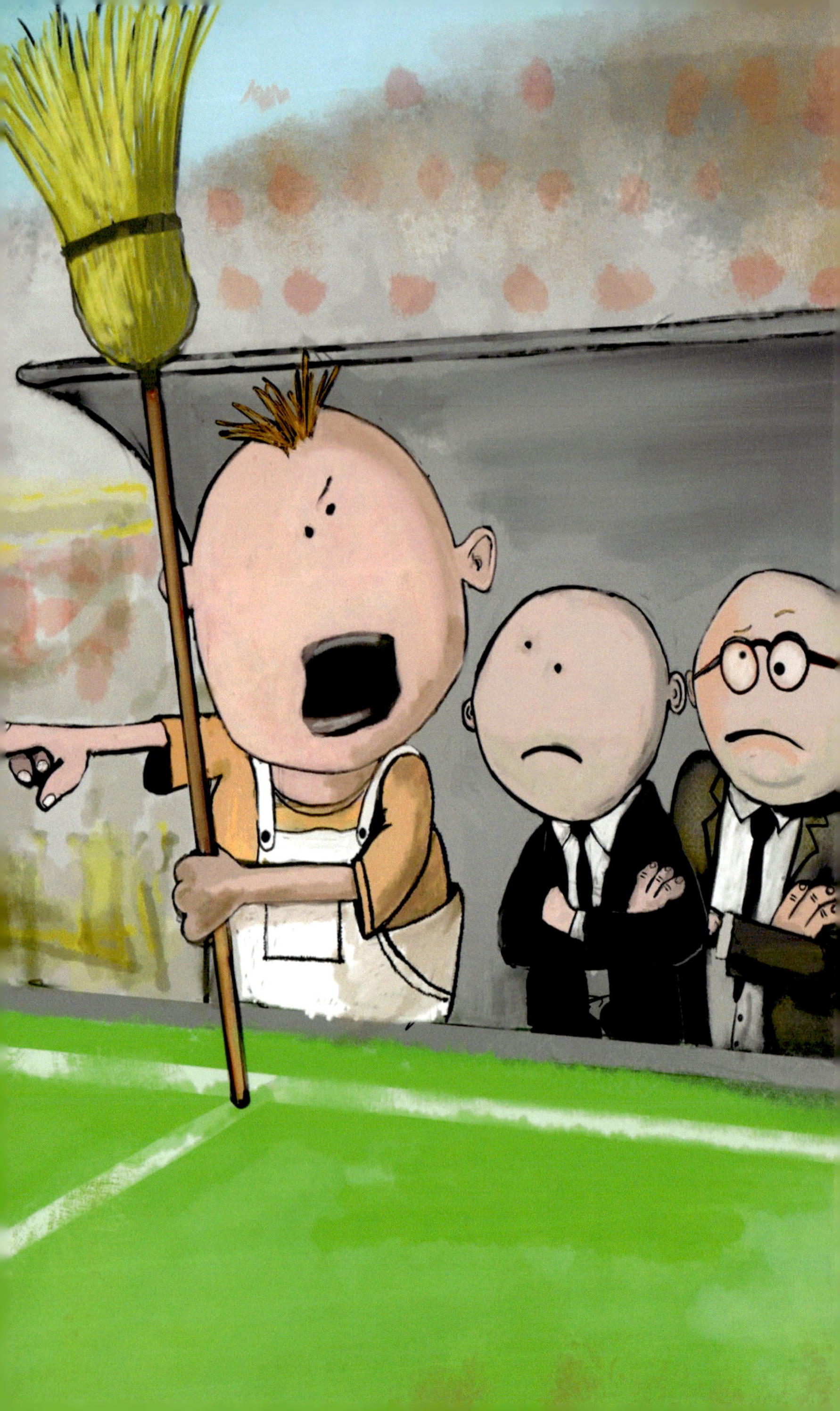

Football

Pass said the coach!

Cross said the manager!

Shoot said the janitor!

Who was asked to leave the dugout.

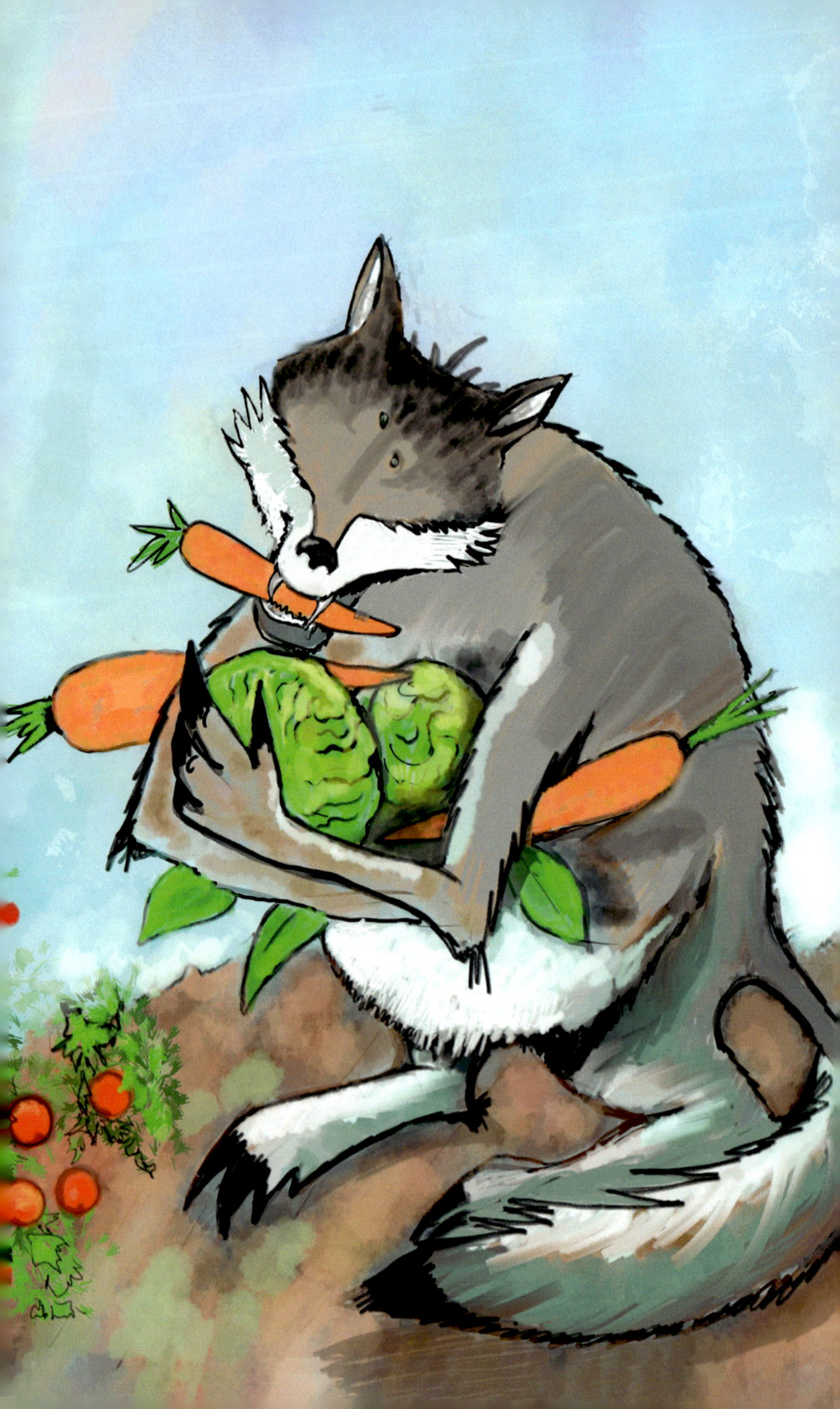

A vegetarian wolf in Gloucester

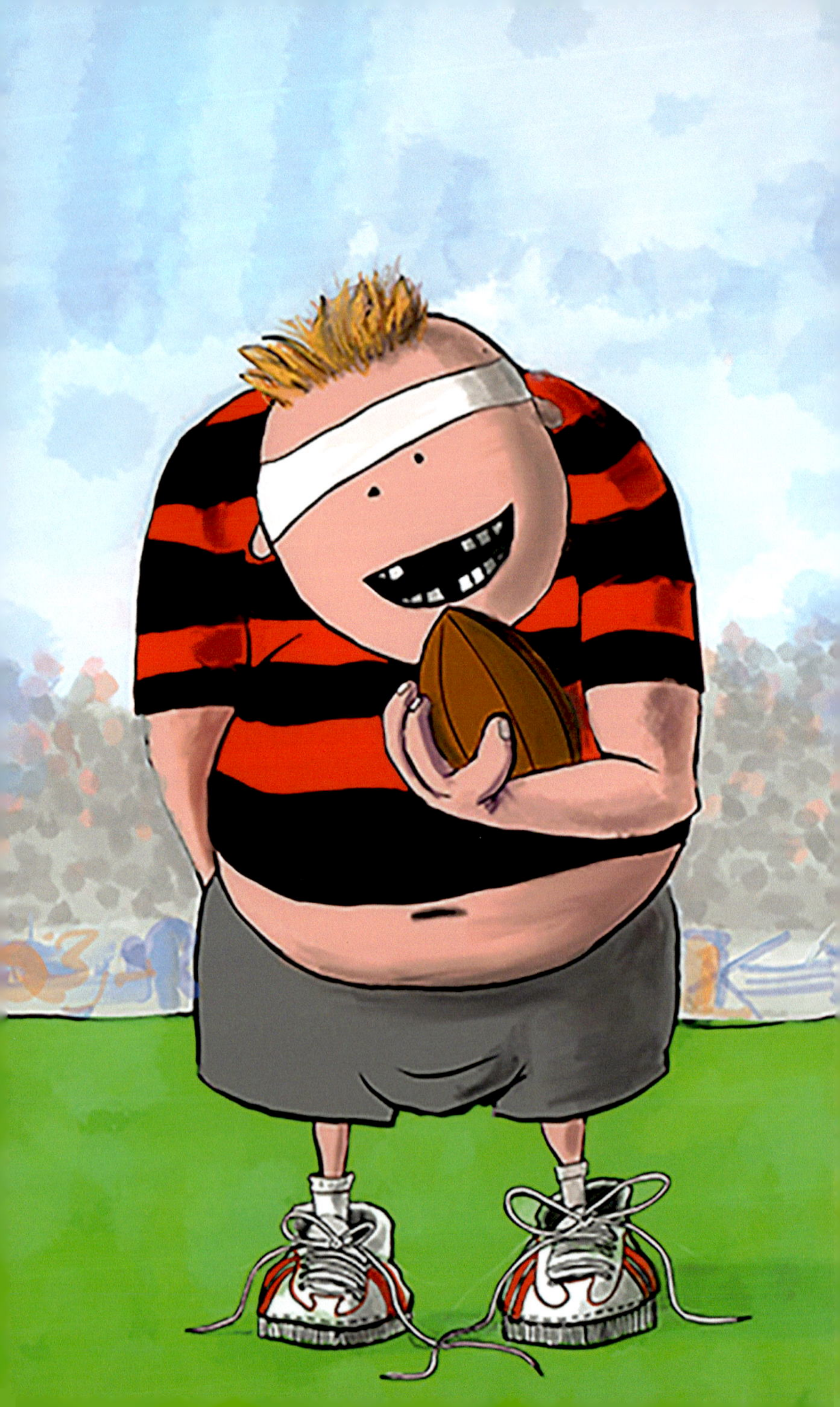

The Rugby Scrum

In the middle of the scrum is the worst place to be.
I was so scared I trickled a little pee.
All the forwards are as big as houses, and as hard as bricks,
It's no place for a back with his good looks and fancy tricks.

The props are shaped like boulders, and have no front teeth.
The number eight is 6ft.12; his name is Kamikaze Keith.
The second-row snort and grunt and drive you in the mud,
One day they got hold of me... Whack, whack, thud, thud.

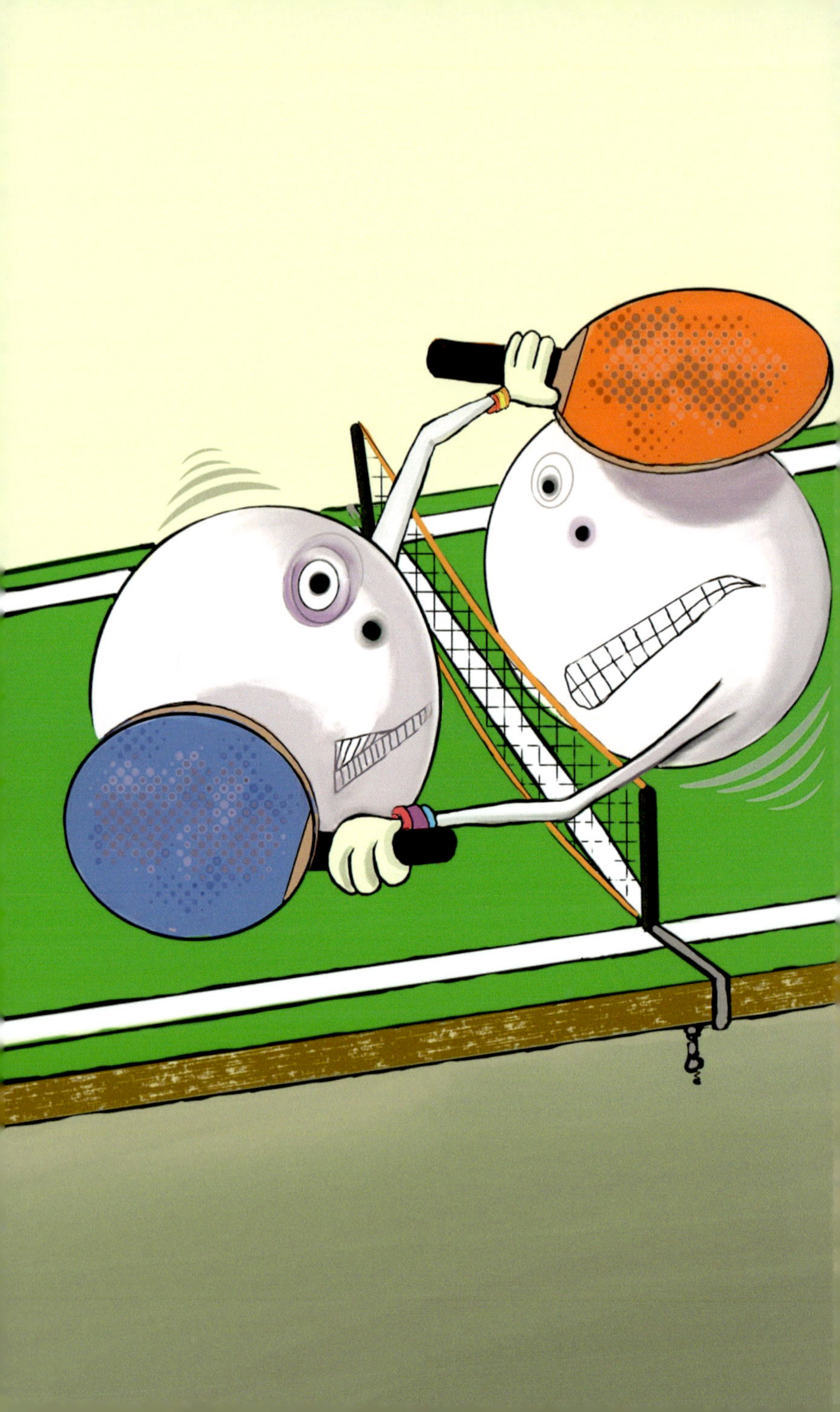

Ping Pong

You have to ping before you pong,
And please don't take too long.
Because the pong won't wait for the ping,
As he is such an impatient thing.

So it's ping, pong, ping, pong,
Ping, pong, ping pong.
And not pong, ping, pong ping,
Because that's a totally different thing.

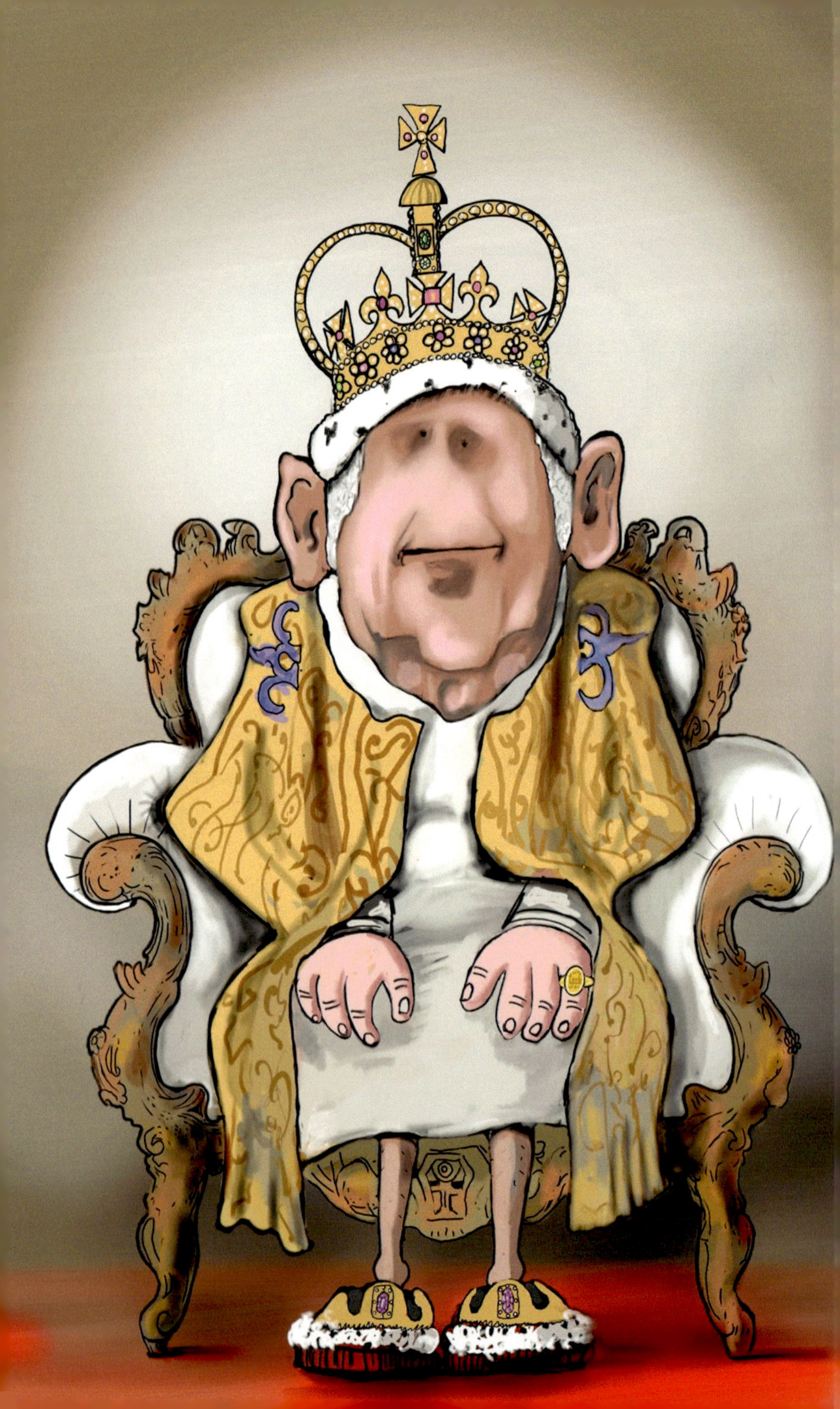

The Kings Coronation

The King sits patiently waiting for his crown.
It's been quite some time in coming say the people in my town.
The rare jewels and diamonds sparkle as it's placed upon his head.
And some nice words are gracefully spoken and said.

Finally our king is crowned with his hat of gold.
It has a hole in the top, I wonder if his head is getting cold?
Appointed by god some claim and dutifully say,
on this bright, sunny, lovely day in May.

But some people don't want a king or to be led,
Maybe that's because his ancestors used to chop off people's heads.

The Potchkin's Alphabet

A was learning the **Alphabet** and stroking fluffy the cat. While...
B Blew up his Balloon and played with his hairy pet rat.
C was having a pee on a tall **Coconut** tree, and the monkeys above all looked shocked.
D was minding his own business, but the monkeys were up to mischief, and **Dropped** a coconut right on his head.
E was **Excited** and purely delighted and laughed with her best friend Fred.
F was **Farting** so much, the bed sheets he clutched, in an effort to stop them blowing away.
G Growled angrily, 'Hey! That smells **Ghastly**, what an awful pong!' As...
H ignored them and continued **Humming** her favourite song.
I took his pill but was still feeling **Ill** and the smell didn't help him at all.

J was **Joyous** and acting rather boisterous while playing with
K and her pink & yellow **Kite**.
L Looked through her books, for a recipe to cook, as
M picked **Mango's** from the trees.
N the **Naughty** mouse, was running around the house, while
O was looking at the beautiful **Ocean** waves.

P Peeled a **Plum** then scratched his itchy bum, and
Q was **Quietly** disgusted.
R was picking **Raspberry's** to make fruit pastries, and
S thought they would be **Simply** divine.
T had lost his **Treasure**, as he had forgotten to measure, how many footsteps he made in the rain.
U who was with him, opened her holey **Umbrella**, but was still getting wetter, which made nothing better at all.
V was on **Vacation** but was left at the station, as a seagull stole her ticket and flew away.
W Watched on and confessed in a song, 'I'm catching...
X-Ray fish in the bay today'.
Y Yelled out loud, 'I've caught a fish and I'm proud!' While...
Z walked his **Zebra** round the town of Jedburgh and happily announced to the world...

'Well done to youuuuuuuuu! You've finished the alphabet and you are as clever as Emma, and a professor, a doctor, a scientist and the prime minister all rolled into one!'

About the Author

This is the first published children's book from James Milligan, son of the renowned author, radio and television personality Spike Milligan KBE. James is 48 years old, lives in Northumberland and has a passion for making people smile and laugh.